Testimonials

"A unique perspective on à great spiritual teacher. Miriam had a front-row seat to the last decade of Swami Kriyananda's life in a way no one else did. She was his personal nurse, traveling the world with him. On many occasions she literally held his life in her hands, as he had given her final responsibility for his medical care, relying on her perfect balance of heart-open devotee and compassionate but impersonal medical professional. Miriam shares many conversations with Swami about death, not as an abstraction but as an imminent possibility to be accepted or — once more — resisted. Humanity and divinity, dancing together. A beautiful, uplifting, extraordinary story. Highly recommended."

—*Asha Nayaswami*, *co-spiritual director of Ananda Palo Alto, and author of* Swami Kriyananda As We Have Known Him *and her most recent book,* Swami Kriyananda: Lightbearer.

"In this inspiring book, we are given an intimate portrait of Swami Kriyananda, a direct disciple of Paramhansa Yogananda, and a great man of God in his own right. Beautifully written by Miriam Rodgers, his personal nurse for the last fourteen years of his life, this portrayal shows us Kriyananda's ability to rise above the severe health challenges he faced and continue to serve others. Through his demonstration of courage and determination, Kriyananda shows each of us the way to face and overcome the tests in our own life. A remarkable window onto the life of a true spiritual hero."

—**Nayaswami Devi**, *co-spiritual director of Ananda Worldwide, and author of* Faith Is My Armor: The Life of Swami Kriyananda

"A brilliant and intimate account of the author's fourteen years with Swami Kriyananda as his cardiac nurse. Each chapter is so lively and vivid that you feel as if you are in the room as everything takes place. There are marvelous little-known stories that give fresh insight into the life of Swami Kriyananda. This is a gem of a book and highly enjoyable reading."

—*Anandi Gray,* licensed clinical counselor, forty-year certified teacher of yoga and meditation, and retired adjunct instructor of philosophy and psychology at Southern Oregon University

"No man is a hero in the eyes of his valet." If you ever wondered about the veracity of this rather disillusioning statement, this book will provide you with page after page of evidence that supports the opposite view. The author's perspective on her subject goes far deeper than how a famous person behaves when they are out of the limelight. For fourteen years, Miriam Rodgers cared for Swami Kriyananda through a series of life-threatening health crises. In her book she gives intimate details of how the high principles that he taught to his audiences around the world were not only lived, but amplified and enhanced by his behavior during the most trying moments of his life. This book provides a source of inspiration for us all."

—*Nitai Deranja,* President, Education for Life International

"In the historic transmission of India's spiritual wisdom to the rest of the world, the contribution of Westerners trained by gurus and yoga masters has been vital. None more so than Swami Kriyananda, whose time with the legendary Paramhansa Yogananda prepared him to be an influential teacher in his own right. The stories of such teachers deserve to be told. In that context, this book is an important addition to the literature of modern spirituality. Not just a biography or a tribute, it is an intimate human portrait, crafted well by someone with a unique point of view as nurse to her subject in the final fourteen years of his life, when legacy, further learning, and spiritual realization mix with the bodily concerns of aging, illness, and impending death. All spiritual seekers will find much to learn in these moving pages."

— *Philip Goldberg, author of* The Life of Yogananda, American Veda, *and* Spiritual Practice for Crazy Times

"A trained cardiac nurse of over thirty years, Miriam was well prepared for the countless medical challenges that Swamiji's body went through. She had the privilege of taking care of Swami's health in the last fourteen years of his life in various places. I have seen the devoted manner with which Miriam took care of Swamiji in Delhi, Italy, and during his many travels to various cities. In this very moving and intimate description of various health crises Swami faced from time to time, she describes how miraculously his life was saved and his indomitable will and courage and faith. This book of Miriam's will be read with great interest by all the admirers of Swami Kriyananda, a remarkable spiritual leader and the most devoted disciple of the great Master Paramahansa Yogananda."

— *D.R. Kaarthikeyan, IPS (R), Former Director, Central Bureau of Investigation; Director General, National Human Rights Commission; and Special Director General, Central Reserve Police Force*

Swamiji

Swamiji

Swami Kriyananda's Last Years
Lessons Learned by His Nurse

~ MIRIAM ROGERS ~

To Swami Kriyananda,
beloved friend and guide
through many lives.
May we be One in that
Light someday.

Crystal Clarity Publishers
Commerce, California
800-424-1055
clarity@crystalclarity.com

ISBN: 978-1-56589-323-8 (paperback)
ISBN: 978-1-56589-593-5 (e-book)
Library of Congress Control Number: 020947320

Cover and interior layout and design
by Tejindra Scott Tully

The *Joy Is Within You* symbol is registered by
Ananda Church of Self-Realization
of Nevada County, California.

Table of Contents

Foreword | ix

Prologue | xiii

Acknowledgements | xvii

1. A Pilgrim's Progress | 3

2. Meeting a Saint | 11

3. A Way of Awakening | 19

4. Endless Bliss | 25

5. Living for God | 33

6. Truth Can Never Die | 43

7. Medjugorje and Divine Mother | 49

8. Circumstances Are Neutral | 59

9. Suffering Is Needed to Find God | 73

10. Seville and a Soulmate | 85

11. Transformative Power | 91

12. Renunciation | 99
Vow of Complete Renunciation | 108

13. Vanished the Veils of Light and Shade | 109

14. The Soul Is Untouched | 115

15. The Final Exam | 119

Epilogue | 129

Further Explorations | 137

Foreword

I served Swami Kriyananda as his personal assistant and caregiver for the last four years of his life. As I look back to that time, and the period leading up to it, I can see that there were a few key people who played a pivotal role in my coming to Swamiji. Miriam Rodgers was one of them.

She was, as you may already know, Swami Kriyananda's nurse. I learned a great amount just by witnessing her dedication to Swamiji, and her behavior towards him. She was to be the first role model in my service to him, and taught me how paying attention to the tiniest of things made such a huge difference in Swamiji's overall well-being. She carried a great responsibility on her shoulders, considering Swamiji's advanced age and turbulent medical history. Yet she always fulfilled it with such humility and attunement; constantly asking Master (Paramhansa Yogananda) to guide her to the right medical course of action in all that she did.

It wasn't easy to balance the outward medical realities with the larger spiritual reality that Swamiji lived in. I felt deep respect for her readiness, always, to adjust to Swami's wishes, and yet be able to find ways to help keep his body going, so that we all could continue enjoying his physical presence for as long as possible.

When Swami's body took unexpected and often sudden turns, Miriam was able to intuitively feel what it was going through. By watching her, I learned not only to understand Swami's body on a physical level, but to perceive how it sometimes needed to burn a specific karma, at which times no medicine or treatment could interfere with that process. The best we could do then was to make him feel as comfortable as possible, and relieve as much pain as we could. It was a daily battle she had to fight, and it took gigantic effort and strength on her part to find that perfect balance.

I remember one afternoon when Swamiji suddenly felt greatly unwell, and decided to go lie down and rest. I felt this urge to check on him just ten minutes later, and to my surprise I found him profusely sweating, his whole body shaking violently. I had no idea what was going on. I immediately phoned Miriam, and she was with us in less than a minute. The moment she saw him she knew: "He is having a hypoglycemic attack! Quickly, bring me a spoon of sugar." She put a big spoonful of sugar into his mouth and helped him get it all down, as Swamiji was barely conscious. A few suspense-filled minutes later he came back.

These were the kinds of episodes we had to be prepared for. Almost daily. Having Miriam around allowed all of us, including Swamiji, to feel relaxed and trust that she would know what do to when the need arose. Swamiji was never afraid, but we, on the other hand, had always to expect the unexpected. His life was in God's hands, and he saw in some of us those hands at work.

At the beginning of our friendship, Miriam would share many things related to Swami's health, which helped me greatly to pray for him, and thereby attune myself to him on a deeper level. Soon we became very close friends. We went through many spiritual crises together, which only reinforced our dedication, commitment, and loyalty to Swamiji, to this path, and to one another, as soul-sisters.

I am eternally grateful for all that she has done, and continues to do, for me and for Swami.

This book contains many stories of Swami's later years and how, on many occasions, he used his own body to expand his guru's work. Each page will reveal to you a picture of what it was to serve someone who had no attachments to his position, his possessions, or even to his own body. His only "attachment" was to do God and Guru's will.

I am sure that the process of writing this book has given Miriam a deeper understanding of what Swamiji truly did for her, and through her. This book is an accurate and revealing account of what Swamiji's later years were about: accelerating people's spiritual progress, fulfilling his guru's mission, and spreading God's Love and Joy wherever he went.

Narayani Anaya
July 27, 2020
Mumbai, India

Prologue

One morning in Assisi, Italy, about a year before he passed away, Swamiji came out of his dining room–office into his living room to meet me for our usual daily checkup. We were both standing, and he looked directly at me and said with great force, "You should write a book." I responded simply, "Okay, Swamiji."

Since his passing in 2013, this commission has stayed with me. I wondered when there would be a chance to start writing the book. Very soon after Swamiji passed, I moved to Ananda Laurelwood in Oregon and began developing retreats and programs at the center there. My five years as the retreat director were quite busy! It was a wonderful experience filled with spiritual growth. I hope those years helped prepare me to write this book about Swamiji.

During the fourteen years I served Swamiji as his nurse, I knew he was showing me something in every moment, modeling the teachings, if only I could grasp them. Often, however, those moments occurred in the middle of a medical crisis with his body. I didn't have time to contemplate the lessons I knew he was offering me. In these years of thinking of my commission to write "the book," I knew that whatever I would share had to express Swamiji's lessons in a universal way that helped everyone. Though I was the one standing in front of him, what he demonstrated was a teaching for all.

People often ask me, "What was it like to be in Swamiji's presence?" There are so many different ways to answer that question that sometimes I don't know where to start.

No matter what was happening, I always felt that Swamiji was completely present. There didn't seem to be any part of him that was mentally somewhere else, either in the past or the future. He gave each person and experience his full attention and acceptance. Whatever was happening around him or to his body, he was calm, centered, and appropriate in his responses. While he could be strong when needed, the hallmarks of his personality were kindness and graciousness.

In Swamiji's presence, I often felt a deep river of creativity flowing through his being. His mind and intellect functioned on a very high level. Books seemed to come through him so easily, as a flow both of creativity and of grace. During his lifetime he wrote a hundred fifty books, several movie scripts, and over four hundred pieces of music. He gave thousands of discourses, authored several plays and novels, and traveled extensively.

Swamiji loved a good laugh. During the time I was with him, almost every afternoon (except for those few weeks before his passing) he would invite some of his close friends to his home for tea. Usually this was a time of lighthearted satsang. Swamiji often liked to get everyone laughing and at ease by sharing a joke. He loved one that Master enjoyed telling: "Her teeth are like stars. They come out at night." No matter how often he shared it, Swamiji was always particularly tickled by it.

My relationship with Swamiji was different from that which he shared with others. Our relationship was not meant to be friendly or social. As his nurse, I was always aware of my responsibility to him, and I had to keep a part of myself utterly objective. Though I was constantly aware of the blessing of being in his presence, and knew he was helping to transform me, I believe Master put a shield or veil between Swamiji and me so that I could not feel the sweet affection for him that others felt. This distance or shield was essential during my years of service to him. It allowed me to be impartial and to make difficult decisions regarding his frequent and challenging health issues. Many of the decisions I had to make were contrary to the opinions of those around him — sometimes even contrary to Swamiji's desires — yet he always honored those decisions and trusted that I knew what needed to be done.

I worried a bit that I didn't feel the affection for Swamiji that others did. But in the final moments of Swamiji's life, Master pierced that veil and I was allowed to experience all of the sweet and dear feelings towards him. As you will read in the final chapter of this book, on the morning of his passing, while sitting at the dining room table, he began to have a small seizure. I wrapped my arms around him to steady him, and I felt him slip out of the body. In that moment, the veil was lifted and the love in my heart for Swamiji flowed out as a great rushing river. I began crying, something I had never done as his nurse, because the love flowing from my heart to his was almost more than I could bear. I knew in the depths of my being that he was my dearest divine friend, and I loved him with all my heart.

Acknowledgements

To Asha Nayaswami, who always encouraged, even insisted, that
I write newsletters and emails during my time with Swamiji.

To Dharana Brown, who helped me find these
countless emails buried in Gmail.

To Maitri Brown, Joy Andreakis, and Aumkara Newhouse
for spending hours listening to me read the first drafts.
Their positive feedback kept me moving forward.

To Dana Andersen, who supported me through the time of
Swamiji's passing and who most emphatically believed
I could write this book. Dana also labored through the initial
editing process and brought needed insights to the stories.

To Anandi Cornell, who did the painstaking job of the
final editing and lent clarity and wisdom to what I'd written.

To Nayaswami Lakshman for his eagle-eye proofreading,
for which Swamiji will be most grateful.

And to my dear husband, David Seybert:
Without his continuous spiritual, emotional, financial, and
joyful support, this book would not have been written.

Swamiji

Swami Kriyananda's Last Years
Lessons Learned by His Nurse

CHAPTER 1

A Pilgrim's Progress

Before finding Swami Kriyananda and Ananda, I had been searching unsuccessfully for my spiritual path for many years. In 1996 my partner gave me *Autobiography of a Yogi* by Paramhansa Yogananda. This book resonated deeply within my soul, and I was especially interested in receiving initiation into Kriya Yoga. But I couldn't understand how to bring what I had read in the book into daily life. Yogananda was an Indian, he had passed away, I lived in the U.S. — how was I to move forward? I started taking the lessons that were offered by Yogananda's organization, Self-Realization Fellowship. But just from reading the lessons, I found it hard to understand the Hong-Sau meditation technique, and I couldn't figure out how to do the Energization Exercises.

In 1998 I was looking for a yoga retreat for my birthday weekend. I called several yoga retreat centers in Northern California, including The Expanding Light Retreat at Ananda Village. A wonderful woman by the name of Jyoti Spearin answered the phone and quickly felt like a friend. I immediately decided to spend my birthday at their

First-Timers' Retreat. That weekend changed my life. I learned how to do the Energization Exercises and also the Hong-Sau technique. The program leaders were Rich and Blanche McCord (now Gyandev and Diksha), who had only recently married and were still adjusting to their new relationship. At meals they regaled us with stories about how they came to marry, and it was a delightful example of how Divine Mother works in our lives. They gave me the address of the Ananda meditation group near my home in Santa Rosa. I started taking yoga classes there and attending the Sunday services. My progress was slow, but I was watchful and open.

Several months after that first visit to The Expanding Light, I had another life-changing experience, on a soccer field. My partner and I played on a coed team every week, and it was during one of the games that I realized something had to change. I came running off the field to the sidelines, in a moment when one would assume that—because of the physical activity and team spirit—I would've been feeling elated and quite happy. But instead, as I stood on the sidelines and looked up at the beautiful blue sky with its fluffy white clouds, I had the very painful realization, "I am so depressed."

What I was experiencing wasn't a psychological condition. In *Autobiography of a Yogi*, Yogananda writes that material life is always dual: rise and fall, pleasure and pain, day and night, and on and on. At a certain point, after a few million births, this "cyclic pattern assumes a certain anguishing monotony." That is what I was feeling deeply—I had hit the wall with the "same old same old" and desperately needed something else.

The Ananda meditation group in Santa Rosa was offering a six-week Raja Yoga class, so I decided to attend it. I thought at least it could help me to meditate twenty minutes a week. Almost immediately, I was easily able to meditate twenty minutes every morning. In just a few days I could meditate twenty minutes twice a day. And by the end of three weeks, I was sitting forty minutes twice a day. Something was happening, and I was going with the flow.

On January 5, 1999, while I was having lunch with a friend, the feeling came very strongly to me that I was to travel to Europe. I was completely surprised by this thought — Europe had never before attracted me. I went to the bookstore for a guidebook to see what was calling me there. I found a thick guidebook to five of the more popular European countries: France, Spain, Germany, Great Britain, and Italy. Just as I was leaving, a smaller guidebook on Italy caught my eye and I bought that also. As I quickly looked through these books at home, it became apparent that Italy was my destination and that this would be a spiritual pilgrimage. Italy seemed like a very spiritual country, with its many majestic cathedrals often containing the incorrupt bodies of saints!

Later that evening, there was a special event at the Ananda meditation center to celebrate Master's birthday. Only later did I appreciate that my inspiration to travel to Italy had come on Master's birthday. As I stood with friends after the event, I told several people about my plan for a pilgrimage to Italy. Someone in the group said, "You know, there's an Ananda center outside of Assisi. You've heard of St. Francis of Assisi?" They also told me that Swami Kriyananda lived in that particular Ananda community. That meant very little to me, as many of my friends at the time were from Self-Realization Fellowship and did not speak highly of Swami Kriyananda. But since I generally don't take the opinions of others too seriously, I was open. That evening I bought Swami Kriyananda's book *The Path*, as well as another book from the boutique. I took these books home and immediately contracted double pneumonia. I couldn't work for the next three weeks. All I could do was lie on the couch reading Swamiji's autobiography and planning my trip to Italy.

I was still intent on receiving initiation into Kriya Yoga. Ananda makes discipleship a requirement for Kriya initiation, so I decided to take the discipleship vow from Ananda on my birthday in February 1999. I thought to myself, "Oh, it's just a vow, but at least it will grant me the Kriya initiation." At the time, I wasn't keen on having a guru. I didn't understand the power of discipleship, and that if I opened myself even a little to this great guru, he was going to take charge of my life. And indeed Master did.

The plan for my one-month Italian pilgrimage included one week each in Rome, Florence, Venice, and Milan. I planned to visit the Ananda center in Assisi over Easter weekend. But Master had other ideas. I arrived in Rome all prepared to play tourist, but Master's voice in my head was loudly saying, "Go to Assisi!" I had only been in Rome for a few days and wasn't due to arrive at Ananda Assisi until the following Easter weekend. But since Master wouldn't leave me alone, I called the retreat center to see if I could come earlier. It was the Saturday before Palm Sunday and they were entirely booked. They told me I could come one day earlier than planned, the following week. I took a deep breath and said, "Are you sure I can't come any sooner?" Then I heard a voice say in perfect English (and no one in that office spoke perfect English), "Tell her to come immediately." I never found out who said those words, but everyone seemed to have heard them because there was a space for me when I arrived.

I left Rome immediately on the next train to Assisi and took a taxi to the Ananda center. Vairagi Escobar, a very dear soul who later became a good friend, greeted me at the front door and took me up

Early days at Ananda Assisi. Here I am (left)with Vairagi, a longtime disciple of Paramhansa Yogananda.

to my room. I sat down on the bed and cried. I was home.

Although I had intended to stay in Ananda Assisi only a few days, I was so inspired by the strong energy and spiritual vibrations there that I stayed for a few weeks. But then the ego got the better of me and decided that we (my ego and I) needed to leave. So I packed everything and left for Florence. I figured I had enough time to see some of Florence and Venice before heading back to Rome and returning to the U.S. as planned.

While in Florence, I found myself constantly losing my way. Normally I have a very good sense of direction, but no matter how many times I would stop a tourist or the police to ask for directions, I would end up wandering around the city lost. Finally, I took this as a message from the universe. I stopped at a sidewalk phone booth to call the reception office at Ananda Assisi and ask if I could come back. They gave me a resounding "Yes!"

I entrained at once for Ananda Assisi, where I remained for al-

Swami Kriyananda as I first saw him, leading a Sunday service in the Temple of Joy in Assisi, Italy.

most two months. I started doing seva (service) in the kitchen and spent lots of time washing dishes. I couldn't understand how such a simple and even monotonous job could give me such profound bliss. I was walking on air and loving every minute of my time there. I began to feel very strongly that this was to be my new home. But the leadership didn't see it that way. They had been asking other American devotees to return to the U.S., as they were trying to make the center primarily for Europeans. Not only was I an American, but I was quite unknown in the world of Ananda.

However, I continued to feel strongly in my heart that I belonged there. I did return to the U.S. to finish things. My partner and I ended our life together. I disposed of everything I owned except what would fit into five pieces of luggage. I received Kriya initiation at Ananda Village ten days before returning to Italy. I arrived at Ananda Assisi as a fresh new Kriyaban and camped in a tent from August through October 1999. I'd found my spiritual path and jumped in with unrestrained enthusiasm!

I took the monthlong ashram training program in November, but was told that as soon as the program was over I would need to live elsewhere. So, for the following four months I lived in various nearby places. Every day I came to the center for morning meditation and then helped prepare lunch in the kitchen so I could be there for breakfast and lunch. I had met Swamiji on my first visit. After he discovered I was a cardiac nurse, he would phone me or invite me over from time to time to check on his health.

The Assisi center closes every January, so I found myself now completely alone. I decided to take my first seclusion retreat and to stay in seclusion for as long as it felt right. During this time I had a birthday. Swamiji did not know I was no longer living at the Ananda center, he did not know I was in seclusion, nor did he know that it was my birthday. But on my birthday my cell phone rang, and the caller ID popped up as "Swami." When I saw the name "Swami," I knew Master was telling me he had not forgotten me. I just needed to hang in there. Swamiji asked me to come over and check his blood pressure. We were sitting in his dining room and when I finished, he became quiet. He leaned back in his chair and just looked at me. I maintained eye contact with him as long as he wished to hold it. I could feel his spiritual power transforming me. No words were spoken, and when it was done, he said his usual goodbye.

During the winter I had been able to stay in various apartments near Ananda Assisi for relatively low prices because it was off season. However, on April 1 all of these places became resort destinations for

9

tourists, and the prices jumped dramatically. I could no longer afford to stay in Italy. I decided to give it all to Master. I told him, "They don't want me at Ananda. If you want me there, you're going to have to make it so." A few days later Kabir MacDow, the Retreat manager, called and invited me to come over for tea and a talk. In this meeting he offered me full-time work as a housekeeper, a place to live, and a stipend. I was delighted beyond measure and immediately moved to the Retreat.

CHAPTER 2

Meeting a Saint

I saw Swami Kriyananda for the first time on Palm Sunday in 1999 at Ananda's retreat center in Assisi. Many of us had gathered in the Temple of Light waiting for him to arrive and give the Sunday service. As he came into the Temple everyone immediately rose to their feet. In walked this obviously very happy and jovial man wearing an orange-colored robe. When he got to the microphone, he immediately began telling all of us (over 100 guests) about the recent surgery on his eyelids. Because his eyelids had begun to droop, obstructing his vision, he'd had to have surgery. Now his face showed the resultant bruises around his eyes and on the side of his face.

I was amazed at how completely relaxed in himself he was, and so transparent and open with everyone there. It seemed as though he had walked into a room with several of his close friends and begun naturally telling them about what had recently happened to him. In the years to come, I learned that Swamiji did indeed see everyone as his friend. Now he was making light of the surgery and, referring to all the green, blue, and purple bruises on his face, ended by saying, "This year, *I* am your Easter egg!" He went on to do the

Sunday service, but the only thing I remember is a man so full of joy and love.

Soon after that retreat, I had wrapped up my life in the U.S. and moved back to Ananda Assisi. After a few weeks in residence, I heard that Swamiji was having problems with his heart beating too fast. I wrote him a quick note letting him know I was a cardiac nurse, and that drinking coffee could cause him to have a fast heart rate and palpitations. I'd learned that, like many of our Italian friends, Swamiji loved cappuccinos and espressos! He immediately made me his nurse and would call me from time to time to come over and check his blood pressure or talk about his medicines. I'd trained for over thirty years as a cardiac nurse in Texas, an intensive care nurse in Berkeley, California, and a home infusion nurse in the Bay Area. In many ways, I'd seen it all, and in those subsequent years as Swamiji's nurse, I was well prepared for the countless medical challenges that Swamiji's body went through.

In the beginning, I was seeing him about once a month for a blood pressure check or other small medical questions. I wasn't managing his medications—he was doing that himself. At one point he mixed up his blood thinner pills and gave himself too many every day for a couple of weeks. This resulted in a minor emergency requiring treatment to stabilize his blood's coagulation. Dr. Peter Van Houten, Swamiji's longtime friend and physician at Ananda Village in the U.S., was consulted and it was decided that I should administer the needed medications to stabilize this episode, as well as check Swamiji's blood coagulation four times a day. This meant I was now in his presence much more than I had ever been before.

Swamiji seemed to have a super-energized state of mind that I thought was due to this overcoagulation of his blood. (I later came

Before a concert at the Temple of Joy with Mangala.

to see that he was often in a superconscious state.) Sometime during the first day of my frequent visits, he launched into a deep spiritual discussion. While in his presence for this lengthy discourse, I couldn't focus on anything he was saying because I was so aware of the spiritual "earthquakes" that were happening inside of me. When I left him, I went immediately to the Shanti Mandir in the basement of the Temple of Light. I tried to meditate, but mostly I was asking Master, "What on earth is happening to me?" I gave up trying to meditate or reason through what was happening. I went in search of someone I hoped could help me.

I found Kabir, who was willing to sit with me and talk about the situation. We went into the woods behind Il Rifugio and sat under some trees. I said to him, "I have no idea what is happening with me now. It's not anything Swamiji is actually saying, but I'm very aware that the soul or the spirit is being deeply moved." Kabir said sweetly, "This is what it's like to be in the presence of a saint." A saint? Up to that point I had not thought of Swamiji as a saint. But when Kabir said those words, they resonated very deeply in my heart. I felt an inner "aha" and with it the thought, "of course." From that point on, I was always keenly aware that I was in the presence of a saint.

Another interesting thing happened during these same days of seeing Swamiji frequently. There were times when Swamiji would become quite curt or short with me, almost as if he were angry about something I had said or done. Once again, I assumed that his state of mind was a reflection of what was happening outwardly. In retrospect, I wonder if he was testing me to see how I would react: Medical professionals need to be impersonal and focused on giving appropriately.

I had recently read the story of Satori, the guru who would seem to become angry with his disciples and throw bricks at them to run them off. One of the disciples carefully collected the brick his guru had thrown at him, took it home, and put it on his altar. The following morning, he discovered the brick had turned to gold.

There was no way I could take Swamiji's behavior toward me personally, since his energy was always impersonal. But I decided to collect some of these "bricks" and take them home and put them on my altar. On three different occasions when I'd been reprimanded, I stopped in the driveway outside his house to collect a rock and put it on my altar at home. I collected a total of three rocks. Over the years I have lost the two larger ones, but I still have the smallest one. It has definitely "turned to gold."

Up to this point in my relationship with Swamiji, I had always called him simply "Swami." Putting the "ji" on the end of his name felt too affectionate. After his blood coagulation had normalized, I needed to continue to see him once a week to make sure his medications were sorted properly. I also began to stay afterwards to clean his house. After a quick check of his blood pressure and medications, he would take off to the nearby town of Assisi with Anand and Kirtani Stickney, the spiritual directors of Ananda Assisi, to do some shopping while I cleaned the house. One morning after I had finished our checkup, Swamiji went into his bedroom to get dressed to go out. I went into the kitchen to get cleaning supplies. As I came out of the kitchen, he was rounding the corner from his bedroom and our paths crossed. We probably paused in this eye-to-eye position for just a split second, but for me, time stood still. In that moment I was shown countless incarnations that I had been with Swamiji. There were lifetimes when he had been my child and I, his mother; others where I had been his wife and he, the husband; but the most important lifetimes were the ones in which I had been his disciple and he was the guru. From that moment on, Swami became Swamiji to me, with all the deep respect and gratitude that suffix expresses.

One evening when Swamiji had developed a high fever and a cough, the Assisi ministers felt they needed to call me to check on him. Although I found him to be quite ill with what was probably rapidly developing pneumonia, I felt no urgency to call the doctor or to do anything medically. He was in bed in his room in Ananda Assisi; Kirtani, Shivani (Lucki), and I were at his bedside. His breathing was labored and noisy, and he did not speak at all for some time. In a strange karmic dance, at one point Shivani would be holding his left hand, I would be at his feet, and Kirtani would be on his right hand. Then in some unspoken way, we would get up and change places. We were praying, but more importantly some karma was being burned. At one point when I was at his feet praying, I had a strong thought that Swamiji was burning my karma. Mentally I said, "O Master, I don't want Swamiji to take on the burden of my karma!

Swami Kriyananda outside the Temple of Joy in Assisi, Italy.

Please give it to me!" Then I heard a very firm and distinct voice say, "You couldn't bear it." So, I let the evening unfold without further mental comment. Finally, at around 2 a.m., Swamiji roused himself and very firmly said it was time to go to bed. He told Kirtani and Shivani to go home but asked me to stay downstairs for the rest of the night.

I think I slept some during the night, but I was awakened around 6 a.m. I wasn't sure what woke me up, but I jumped out of bed and ran upstairs to check on Swamiji. In my urgency, I burst through the door into his living room. I hit a wall of complete silence and stillness. It was as though all the molecules in the room had ceased vibrating. I could see through the dim light of dawn that Swamiji was sitting upright in one of his chairs meditating. There was not a sound in the room; the usual loud ticking of the clock and the refrigerator motor were silent. I could not hear Swamiji's breathing. Just a few hours earlier you could hear his ragged breathing from across the room. Swamiji was in the breathless state. As quietly as I could, I backed out of the room, went downstairs, and attempted to meditate. I very much wanted to tune in to what was happening upstairs, but I don't think I came anywhere close in my distracted and awestruck state! Sometime later I heard Swamiji cough and knew he had finished his meditation. I went upstairs, and acting as though nothing unusual had happened, we started the day by calling the doctor to get Swamiji treatment for his pneumonia.

CHAPTER 3

A Way of Awakening

In October 2003 in Assisi, Swamiji had just finished the final touches on his newest book, *Conversations with Yogananda*, when a couple showed up from India to meet with him. Although they were Americans, they had been living in India for some years. They told Swamiji that Master's work in India was almost nonexistent, or at least quite dormant. Swamiji had long felt that Master wanted him to go back to India someday to continue to build the work he'd started there in 1958. Swamiji took this meeting as a sign from Master, and immediately started making plans to move to India. In less than a month, Swamiji had rallied the troops—calling longtime friends with whom he'd built the work in America—and they were already in India scouting out places to live. Swamiji was on his way to bring his guru's mission back to his homeland.

Soon after arriving in India and establishing a home base in Gurgaon, just outside New Delhi, Swamiji was approached by an Indian TV station asking if he would make several twenty-minute shows to air on a spiritual channel. Swamiji immediately realized the blessing in this offer. At his age, traveling extensively throughout India to give lectures as he had in his youth would be extremely difficult. But through the medium of TV, he could reach millions every day.

Swamiji decided to use his newest book, *Conversations with Yogananda*, as the basis for these TV shows, which he called, "A Way of Awakening." Each show featured a twenty-minute talk by Swamiji based on one of the conversations, and ended with one of his songs. Nirmala Schuppe, then the co-spiritual director of Ananda India, worked with Swamiji to help him decide which of the conversations to use for his talks, and which song would go with each talk. The songs recorded for this project became the *Philosophy in Song I* and *II* albums. Swamiji decided to do 365 shows, so the preparation alone was a great undertaking.

Swamiji began recording the shows sometime in April or May. The recording sessions were "on again, off again," on account of his many other projects, and due also to health issues. In April 2004 Swamiji had to be admitted to the local hospital ("Privat") due to congestive heart failure. While in the hospital with him, I received a call informing me that my mother was dying. When Swamiji asked me what was happening, I said, "Swamiji, I don't want to go." I felt my place was with him and in service to Master's new work in India. Swamiji accepted my choice to stay and we said no more about it. My mother did not pass away at that time.

In November 2004, Swamiji committed the entire month to finishing the TV recordings, which meant he had to record at least ten shows a day. Although Swamiji's spirit was always willing, the body did not make it easy for him. He was extraordinarily exhausted throughout this month of recording. It was remarkable to see him in the morning barely able to raise his spoon to eat his breakfast. Then, just minutes later, in front of the camera he delivered talk after talk from inspiration, all of them powerful and profound discourses on Master's teachings.

I had the great blessing of sitting right next to the camera to reset the timer and hold the sign telling him which song would be sung at the end of a particular talk. Anyone who wanted to come and be in the room (we were filming in the living room of the house where he lived) was welcome to attend. However, you had to be able to stay awake and alert! Gurgaon is very hot that time of year, and when the cameras were rolling, klieg-type lights were on and the (noisy) air conditioner needed to remain off. Swamiji occasionally banished someone from the room because of a head nodding off. Oh, the shame! Swamiji needed the full, energetic support of everyone in the room.

For me, this was a transforming experience in that I, too, had to keep my energy very high. I had to keep my focus at the spiritual eye and not let my energy waver for a moment. My concentration had to be single-pointed, which was not easy for the wild pony that lives in my mind. I experienced a great deal of grace throughout to allow me to do this.

Swamiji on set in Gurgaon.

I took notes during the recordings (this is one way to stay awake!). Here are some snippets of Swamiji's wisdom.

Conversation #325: Swamiji was having trouble getting the results he wanted in meditation. He found a moment alone with Master and told him that he was trying and trying but unable to go deep. He asked, "Am I not trying hard enough?" Master shook his head and said, "You are trying too hard." He told Swamiji to emphasize relaxation. Swamiji explained that in meditation we must get ourselves out of the way, so that the Infinite can fill us. He went on to say, "Suspend thought in total absorption. When the mind is still, thoughts are impossible. Deep meditation is a death experience."

Conversation #333: Master was talking to a group of disciples about Sister Gyanamata, who had recently passed. The last twenty years of her life had been a continuous experience of physical suffering. Master explained, "The body is only a plate. Eat the feast of spirit from it, as she did, while you still have the body. After that, what happens to the plate no longer matters." As Swamiji elaborated on this conversation, he said that we must be grateful for everything, including all suffering, because the Guru is working out all our karma. He went on to say, "The closer we are to God, the more frequently the tests come, because we no longer push them away. Detachment does not mean apathy. The more we can act without likes or dislikes, the more inner joy we will experience."

Conversation #393: Master said, "Don't be emotional when you pray. At the same time, don't be diplomatic. God is like a little child. You don't need to be tactful with Him. Talk to Him earnestly, with calm confidence. Tell him sincerely how you really feel." Swamiji went on to discuss the purpose of yoga, which he said is to achieve a higher state of prayer. "Go beyond all form. If you see Divine Mother, look into Her eyes, see that consciousness. To those without peace, how can joy come? Seek the Mother's love."

In Conversation #402, Master said, "It is difficult to find one's way out of the labyrinth. In one of the Greek legends, Theseus slew the Minotaur, which was at the center of a labyrinth. Ariadne gave him a thread to unreel as he entered the labyrinth. That thread enabled him to retrace his steps and find his way out. The thread symbolizes the guru's advice, and your inner attunement with him. Even mental attunement will suffice to lead you to freedom. By that sacred thread, you will be led by God's grace." Swamiji added, "Inner attunement is more important than the techniques. You need a guru because his consciousness can go subtly into your own and help dispel maya. Inner and outer attunement is how this subtle consciousness can come into us. I always ask my Guru what to do. I have been willing to give him everything, even my life."

Conversations #403 and #412: Master talks about chanting. He often said, "Chanting is half the battle." Master would chant until he had an experience of God. Swamiji said, "When you chant to God, you are getting in touch with the divine AUM. Through chanting you can commune with AUM and merge into it. Chant loudly at first to engage the mind, then more and more softly. When you come into ecstasy, there is no outward sound. The goal of chanting is to put you into relationship with the Divine."

~ ~ ~ ~ ~ ~ ~ ~ ~ ~

With Nirmala and Swamiji.

In mid-November, while Swamiji was recording the "Way of Awakening" TV shows, I received word that my mother had passed. Swamiji too was informed. When I greeted him that morning before the filming started, he offered his condolences and said he was praying for my mother. He also told me that she was blessed to have me as a daughter. I replied that she was very blessed to have him praying for her. Nothing more was said. I had no plans to leave Swamiji and go to her funeral. She had had Alzheimer's for a long time, and had not recognized me for the last four years. Swamiji knew my karma was not to take care of her or even to attend her funeral, but rather to help him serve Master's work. This was unusual, but it was also exactly right.

Swamiji finished all 365 TV shows. They aired nightly on the Aastha TV channel for some years and reached millions in India, as well as many in Southeast Asia and the USA.

CHAPTER 4

Endless Bliss

Swamiji seemed to live in a constant state of bliss, no matter what was happening to the body. If you were sensitive, you could feel that bliss. He would often say that he could no longer practice Kriya. Since his heart surgery many years earlier, his heart almost always had been in atrial fibrillation. This means the upper chamber quivers rather than contracts rhythmically. He said it felt like having a washing machine in his chest, and it was impossible for him to become still in meditation. However, many times when I walked into Swamiji's living room, I would find him sitting in one of his comfy chairs in what appeared to be meditation, and he was most obviously in a state of bliss. He would remain oblivious to our quiet movements in the room. Lila, his cook of many years, might come in to set the table for breakfast and I would be preparing the morning medications and tidying the room. But Swamiji was with God and nothing else existed.

One of the most stunning experiences I had of Swamiji's constant state of bliss happened one day when he had begun writing Master's commentaries on the Hindu scripture the Bhagavad Gita.

Swamiji had been with Master in his desert retreat at Twenty-Nine Palms when Master wrote his commentaries on the Bhagavad Gita. Since Master had told him that his work was lecturing, writing, and editing, Swamiji assumed he would someday edit Master's commentaries on the Gita. However, Swamiji was thrown out of his Guru's organization ten years after Master left his body, and he could no longer access any of Master's original manuscripts. For many years Swamiji was in a quandary as to how he could possibly edit Master's commentaries without them.

In India in the fall of 2005, Swamiji was once again feeling a strong desire, an urgency, to write the commentaries on the Gita. But how could he possibly do it without the original manuscript? He thought back to a dream he'd had years earlier, in which Yogananda had appeared to him. In the dream, Swamiji shared his longing to edit the Gita commentaries and his inability to work from the original. Master told him, "Don't overlook the possibility of a skylight." Swamiji decided he could at least rewrite the slokas, as these have been translated numerous times from Sanskrit. He felt he could express them more succinctly and clearly than earlier translators, and in a way that reflected Yogananda's understanding of them. The work on the slokas flowed easily and quickly for him.

As he worked on the slokas, memories came to him of Master's words as he'd dictated his commentaries years earlier in the desert. In fact, Swamiji realized that he was able to remember, not word for word, but rather concept by concept, exactly what Master had said.

Finally, on October 14, the commentary itself burst forth! First, Swamiji assembled thirty pages of introduction to the Gita with thoughts he had shared in previous books. Then he began writing the new material, interpreting the Gita itself with what he remembered of Master's commentaries. In minutes, he had over six pages for us to read. It was a thrilling moment! He began writing at least ten pages a day of Gita commentaries. He understood now what Master had meant by a "skylight": The inspiration was flowing effortlessly from above. The joy in the house was positively palpable.

Very early in this process, perhaps around the third or fourth day of intense writing, I went to Swamiji's bedroom before dinner, to treat his painful shoulder with a special penlight. He was seated in his comfy chair with the most beatific smile on his face. He had no book or papers in his lap as he usually did, but was simply sitting, in the most apparent bliss.

He began talking of the Gita and also of leaving his body. He had often spoken of leaving the body—to him it seemed quite desirable since his body had so many challenges and he was "tired of being tired." But this time was very different. His face was filled with a beautiful peachy glow that he would get when he was full of Master's presence. He kept looking upward, at the door or ceiling—not at me. He spoke with such sweet yearning for the time when he would die, as though he was eagerly anticipating a divine vacation with Master. Swamiji said that he knew he must complete the Gita commentaries and that Master was using him to do this. He said he was happy to let this body be used to burn karma, his or others. I wish I remembered more precisely what he said, but what was conveyed was much more than the words. I don't normally see visions, but as I sat with Swamiji, I saw a faint yet powerful downpour of golden rain suffusing the entire room. I could hardly see his face for all these golden shafts of light.

Swamiji's health took a deep plunge during those first few weeks of writing. His blood sugars were higher than ever, blood pressure was up, ankles were swollen, heart racing, and all without apparent cause. His health had been very stable in the previous weeks. The only reason we could come to was the stress of writing this great scripture. Swamiji would often say, "I'm scared to death of this work." Master had said the Gita commentaries would "bring millions to God." What a weight of responsibility Swamiji felt! He said he feared he would not be able to remember well enough what Master had written in the original manuscript. But as the days went by, the words continued to flow uninterruptedly, at a steady pace of ten to twelve pages a day.

Swamiji was so full of joy as, several times a day, he went up and down the three flights of stairs between his office and the living room with "hot off the press" pages for us to read. He was always enthusiastic for someone to read the newest pages, so we tried to be constantly available. What a blessed time for everyone on staff and all of our visitors who came over daily to read the manuscript.

Swamiji's health stabilized, and although he was very tired at the end of each day, he was glowing. There was such a deep feeling of love in his presence. I had never known that love could be seen, but there it was in Swamiji, clear enough to touch.

One night, Swamiji said that he could feel Master's bliss flowing through him, and indeed, we could see it and feel it. But there was something more. I said to him that night, "It feels like Master is living in this house now." Swamiji said, "Oh, yes!" And that was it. You could just about *see* Master with his orange robes streaming behind him running down the stairs alongside Swamiji — both of them excited with each new page.

Swamiji was quite busy with many visitors during those two months, but somehow he managed to write at least ten pages of Gita commentaries every day. It was a time of incredible joy. Somewhere around the fortieth day of writing, Swamiji came with his newest ten pages.

This is an excerpt of what he wrote:

(10:8) I am the Source of everything. From Me all creation emerges. Realizing this great truth, the wise, awe-stricken, adore Me.

What is awe-inspiring about Supreme Truth is not the sheer number of its manifestations—which are, indeed, beyond numbering—but its cascade of overwhelming bliss.

When I read this passage, I remembered my experience in Swamiji's room on that special day. What looked to me like golden rain, I believe, was a "cascade of overwhelming bliss."

Swamiji finished his commentaries on the Gita in only sixty-one days. The manuscript required very little editing and stands as his *magnum opus*.

~ ~ ~ ~ ~ ~ ~ ~ ~ ~

Often after finishing a project, Swamiji would take a vacation to celebrate with Divine Mother. If he was in India, his preferred destination was Goa, located on the west coast of India and in the south. He liked to stay at a particular hotel called the Taj Exotica because it offered a community-like ambiance. He most especially liked the way the guestrooms were arranged on the property. Each building contained just four: two upstairs, and two down. Lovely walkways ran between the various guest buildings, and Swamiji could easily walk from his room to the restaurants or shopping areas. The staff

Swami Kriyananda presenting the finished Gita, his magnum opus.

always treated Swamiji as if he was a dear friend, and they were delighted to have him visit. There were lovely shops located within the main building — and Swamiji loved to shop!

Once while in Goa, Swamiji was enjoying dinner in the usual fashion with some close friends. Then suddenly he stopped eating and sat back in his chair. We all could tell he was going to say something, so the table got quiet. He looked around at all of us, and said, "Sometimes I feel so much bliss, I can hardly stand it." He became choked up and a little teary on the word *bliss*. Bliss — the experience and even just the word — seemed to evoke in him profound gratitude. It was amazing to see an entire table of boisterous, talkative people suddenly become very interiorized devotees.

Swamiji had bought an extraordinarily beautiful painting of Krishna right before going to the restaurant. He had spent some time gazing at it before leaving the store. Perhaps it was this that elicited that "overwhelming cascade of bliss" that came over him at dinner.

CHAPTER 5

Living for God

Swamiji heard Master say on more than one occasion, "Living for God is martyrdom!" Often it seemed that we were waiting in the Garden of Gethsemane with Swamiji. Waiting and praying with him before the next Passion was revealed.

It was now May 2007, and Swamiji was back in Italy. Since December, he had been having acute episodes of Ménière's disease; it had been a roller-coaster ride of ups and downs with his physical health. Ménière's is a condition of the inner ear that causes a person to experience vertigo, tinnitus, motion sickness with accompanying nausea and diarrhea, and profound weakness. The symptoms can strike at any time with little or no warning. Traveling in a car or an airplane aggravates the symptoms, and due to his travel schedule, Swamiji was frequently in cars or planes. Unfortunately, there is very little that can be done by way of effective treatment.

Despite the challenges with the body in the previous five months, Swamiji had accomplished all that he set out to do in Italy and more. Now it was May 19, his birthday. The night before, in Rome, there had been a very successful book launch of *The Essence of the Bhagavad*

Gita. On the morning of his birthday we drove from Rome to Assisi; by the time Swamiji arrived at his birthday banquet in the afternoon, he had already put in a full day. The motion from the car ride had turned his equilibrium completely upside down. With Ménière's, the brain doesn't know which way is up, so it doesn't send signals to the muscles in the legs or body to maintain him in an upright position.

In addition to having bad nausea and diarrhea, Swamiji also could not stand or even hold his head up for long. Yet there he was at his birthday banquet, greeting and blessing hundreds of people. When he could no longer sit upright, Jyotish Novak and D.R. Kaarthikeyan escorted him out of the dining room. By the time he had walked from the dining room to his car, he was leaning way over with his feet stretched out behind him, his head hanging down on his chest, and his hands holding tight to Jyotish and Kaarthikeyan's arms. It had to be the saddest thing any of us had ever seen. Many of us burst into tears. This was our Swami and he seemed to be suffering so much. He seemed like Jesus carrying a heavy cross up to Calvary. But as he neared the car, he lifted his head and looked up into the crowd. There was this great big smile on his face and his eyes radiated pure bliss. Then we *really* wept. Tears of pity turned to tears of immense joy and gratitude. Swamiji is not his body. He was untouched by what the body was experiencing.

In 2008, Swamiji was diagnosed with cancer. (The full story is told in Chapter 8.) We were with him in the hospital in Delhi the night before he was to receive his first round of chemotherapy. He told us he had just relived his childhood experience with colitis, a time of tremendous pain and nausea. He was afraid he would have to go through the same experience for the next four months of chemo. He said to his doctors and to us that his courage had failed him, and he was frightened. One could almost hear the words, "Father, let this cup pass from me." However, by morning we could clearly feel his resolve, "Thy will be done."

By early 2009, Swamiji had made it through the cancer surgery and chemotherapy in India; now we were preparing to leave for Italy, where he had a long list of events scheduled. He was rapidly approaching the birthday that was predicted by the Book of Bhrigu to mark the end of his life. In our last weeks in India, Swamiji invited a number of friends to come by for tea. He shared with them that this might be his final goodbye.

Often, when Swamiji was about to travel to another community where he would lead many important events, his health would start to fail. He would say that it was Satan trying to prevent him from doing what he had come to do. Now, again, as we were preparing to leave India, small things started to go wrong with the body. And then bigger things started to happen. Swamiji seemed to be having "small strokes." Because he had told me many times that he felt these illnesses were from Satan trying to prevent him from carrying on his mission, I felt strongly that, even with the small strokes, we had to get him on the plane to Italy. Swamiji knew I would not try to stop him from doing what he had planned to do and therefore trusted my decisions. Also, we had an agreement that I would not admit him to a hospital unless it was absolutely necessary. I could handle most of his medical care at home, and so, with Dr. Peter's input, I increased his blood thinner medication. "A day or so before I left India," Swamiji later wrote,

> I was watching a DVD, and suddenly everything went black for an instant. Seems like a mild stroke. The next

day (I think it was), as I was getting ready to fly out, I found I couldn't remember perfectly simple things; I was extraordinarily weak, and mentally fuzzy. Still, I took the plane. I went through London, but by the time I reached Lugano (Switzerland) I could only be described as weaker.

By the time we reached Lugano, it had become clear that Swamiji was having small strokes and we needed to do more for him medically. Swamiji relied on me not only to be a nurse for the body, but also his divine bodyguard supporting him in the battle. Decisions were often made that might have seemed strange or even negligent to those on the outside. My role was to support him in his chosen battle and his work in the world. We didn't take him to the hospital in Lugano, but instead called on other resources. Dr. Donatella Caramia, a neurologist and close friend of Swamiji's in Rome, consulted with her colleagues; they all agreed that Swamiji should be given aspirin to help augment the effectiveness of the blood thinner. This definitely seemed to help, and the stroke symptoms went away. But now Swamiji's body experienced hemorrhages of countless small blood vessels throughout his body. His arms, legs, and torso all became covered with dark bruises.

At this point, it was very important to check Swamiji's blood work, and particularly to perform his coagulation studies. A dear friend of ours in Lugano, Simone Stefanini, a veterinarian, was able to obtain the lab supplies we needed to do a blood draw. Because of Swamiji's badly swollen arms, I knew I would not be able to access the one tiny vein in his right arm that generally worked for blood draws. Simone was used to accessing little veins in the forelegs of small animals, and I felt confident that he could successfully draw Swamiji's blood. When we entered Swamiji's hotel room and I told him that Simone was going to be drawing his blood, Swamiji became irate. I had always been able to do a good job of drawing his blood, and he insisted that I should do it now. But I knew in that moment I would be unsuccessful, so I insisted that Simone draw the blood. Swamiji then said in a very snooty British accent, "I've been reduced to a veterinarian." It seemed he was trying to make a tense moment lighter. Simone was easily able to draw the blood sample; when he finished, Anand, who had been standing quietly in the room watching all of this, said, "Swamiji, you can bark now!" Simone and I were relieved to have the mood lighten up a bit, but Swamiji was not amused.

Because of this hemorrhagic event, more complications came along: congestive heart failure and severe anemia. Swamiji spoke about the possibility of leaving his body. He would lie on the bed with his arms outstretched and say, "I feel like I'm fading away." I well knew he was in critical condition and the body could easily succumb, but, strangely, I never felt Swamiji would die. Still, it was imperative that I keep my energy high and offer his body as much medical support as possible.

The stress I felt in the situation was increased because there were many strong and diverse opinions about how to handle Swamiji's medical care, primarily among his good friends. Some thought I was panicking and overreacting. Then, the next day, some of them were overreacting and wanting to whisk Swamiji to the hospital. Master used to say we must be able "to stand unshaken amidst the crash of breaking worlds." In this case, I felt he was teaching me to stand unshaken amidst the clash of differing opinions.

Fortunately, during this time Narayani and I were sharing a small room at the Acquarello Hotel, next door to the Dante Hotel, where

Swamiji was staying. Narayani would sit and meditate for hours while I wrote e-mails or spoke with Dr. Peter on the phone. She continually supported me and helped me move through this stressful process. Swamiji had three major things wrong with the body, any one of which warranted a hospitalization. And he was in a hotel in Lugano, with no one but me and Simone, a veterinarian, to take care of him. Of course, it was priceless to be able to consult with Dr. Peter by phone.

Narayani and I often found ourselves meditating at midnight, because that's when my day could stop for a few hours. We were always up at 5 a.m. for morning meditation. She helped me keep my sanity. As stressful as it was, it was also amazingly blissful. We both had a strong sense that Swamiji was going through something profound, and we considered ourselves deeply blessed to be with him to witness it.

We felt we were watching the Passion of Christ: the scourging, the long walk to Calvary followed by the Crucifixion, and (we hoped) the Resurrection. Though the Coumadin combined with aspirin had saved Swamiji from a full-blown stroke, now his arms were solid black from the resultant hemorrhaging. He had hematomas all over his body, including some fairly large ones on his lower legs.

Because of his critical condition, we could not fly Swamiji from Milan to Assisi. Instead we had to drive him back to his home. There, he had to have someone with him twenty-four hours a day. Anand usually stayed overnight. Asha was also with us, helping with Swamiji's care.

Some of the procedures I had to do for Swamiji were quite uncomfortable. He had an implantable port under the skin on his chest, into which I had to put a large-bore needle with, for example, iron injections for his severe anemia. This procedure is extremely painful;

he often winced when I did it and it left him kind of shaky. A few mornings after we arrived in Assisi from Lugano, I again had to do this procedure. I saw a momentary resistance flash across his face, but this was immediately followed by a complete acceptance of what was happening. He even started to hum a little tune. After I took the needle out and knelt in front of him holding pressure over the site, he looked at me and started crying. He said, "At times, I feel so much bliss, I can hardly stand it."

For some days, Swamiji remained almost completely bedbound. Then, astonishingly, just a few days before his upcoming events in Rome, Swamiji got out of bed and completely dressed himself. He walked into the living room where Anand, Asha, and I were gathered, and said he had been resurrected. Babaji had assured him that he would live probably another ten years. Though he was not thrilled about the idea of another ten years in the body, he said he felt he had been through the Crucifixion and Resurrection. He said that he believed that it was Master's will that brought him through. He clarified his statement by repeating that it was Master's *will*, rather than Master's *grace*.

The morning of Swamiji's instantaneous healing, he began to speak of creating a new swami order. As he discussed his new vision for the future of Ananda, only Anand, Asha, and I were present. This new renunciate order was to open the door to formal renunciation for more people. That morning he looked at Anand and said, "This new order is for you." Anand stuttered, explaining that he was married. Swamiji clarified that this renunciate order could include householders.

Stepping back from that thrilling morning of Swamiji's resurrection, I have to say that, from a medical standpoint, he shouldn't

Swamiji sending the blessing of AUM out to all the world.

have survived the episode in Lugano. In the ten years I'd been caring
for him, I had never before seen him so critically ill. But through the
whole experience, I had the overpowering feeling that he was going
through yet another Passion. I don't know how many others were
aware of the miracle we were witnessing, but you could find Asha
sitting at Swamiji's feet at every possible moment.

It felt as if we had been on the road to Calvary with Swamiji and witnessed the Crucifixion. Swamiji used these words to many of us privately, though not in his letters to others. It truly felt as though he had been completely reborn or resurrected. His color was that beautiful peachy glow, and he walked easily, unassisted. In an email at this time he wrote that inspiration and activity seemed to be rushing through him like a great torrent. He spoke again about the spiritual transformation he felt he had undergone through his experience in Lugano. He felt his miraculous survival was through Master's *will*.

A few days after recovering from this medical crisis, Swamiji was able to do a satsang in the Temple of Light at Ananda Assisi. We were deeply moved as he shared his own experience of the love of God. The Temple was full to overflowing and many were weeping with Swamiji. When he held up his arms to show that they were almost completely black from the ecchymosis, all I could think of was "stigmata."

CHAPTER 6

Truth Can Never Die

When I first came to Ananda Assisi, I had read Swami Kriyananda's autobiography, *The Path*; I was also aware of the court case in which allegations of sexual misconduct had been aimed against him. On my first trip to Ananda Assisi in 1999, I stayed in the retreat center as a guest. As I've mentioned earlier, I was thrilled by the high vibrations. But I had questions about this court case and wondered who in the community could help me.

One young man (who later became my husband) told me that he had been in Ananda Palo Alto during many of those court case years; he had learned quite a lot from the legal team, read some of the depositions, and felt he understood fairly thoroughly what had taken place. During our long talk, he candidly answered my many questions.

Discovering the actual facts of the lawsuit was a turning point for me. I'd been considering becoming a part of Ananda, and this conversation helped me make the decision. I had already met Swami Kriyananda, and to me he seemed utterly transparent. He was himself being himself. If he could slip as he had, and then pick himself up and continue steadfastly towards his goal of God-realization, there was hope for me. He was obviously a man of great integrity and nobility, and I decided in that moment to follow him and become actively involved in all aspects of Ananda.

As in the case of most saints, Swamiji experienced much persecution in his life. He was thrown out of his guru's organization; he was subjected to twelve years of litigation in two different lawsuits in the U.S. and another five-year court case in Italy. Throughout all these experiences, Swamiji's faith was untouched and his love for God never wavered.

In 2006, while living in India, Swamiji was approached by a local talk show and asked to be a featured guest for a segment about "how India's spiritual practices have declined in some ways from what they once were, and what could be done going forward to improve matters. It would be a constructive discussion about how to improve India's spiritual life." We were told it was being done in honor of Sri Satya Sai Baba's birthday, but he wasn't to be the main topic. The TV station managers had come to our ashram to invite Swamiji, and they seemed like nice people. Our Indian friends said this was a popular show. So we went for it.

On the morning of the taping, Swamiji started the day with unusually high blood sugar. Not bad, but high for him in relation to the previous few weeks. We had to leave the house right after breakfast, and he was obviously not feeling well. On the way to the studio, he complained of dizziness and nausea, then broke out in a cold sweat; he was on the verge of fainting, and the car had to be pulled over so he could vomit. This made him feel somewhat better, but he was very weak. He insisted on going through with the talk show.

When we arrived at the studio, Swamiji was not steady on his feet. After sitting down for a short time, he suddenly lost all hearing

Thank you, Swamiji!

in his right ear. We thought the battery had gone dead in his hearing aid. (In retrospect, we know he was having a small stroke.) Somehow, he pulled himself together and we were taken into the studio to begin taping. All the featured guests and the audience sat on bleacher-like seats in a big circle. The studio had huge columns of red and white lights against a black background. We didn't know it at the time, but we'd entered hell.

Nothing they had told us about the show was true. They began trying to discredit many of the spiritual leaders in India and especially Sai Baba, who was characterized as a "miracle monger."

The talk show host asked Swamiji, "What is your view on miracles?" Swamiji said, "I think it's all a play of maya [delusion]. Miracles can happen and what does it mean if they happen? Sai Baba materialized a little mala as a gift for me, it was very sweet. Maybe it was a real miracle, maybe it wasn't. I don't care! I think: Who is God? Is he God? No. Everybody is God. Nobody is special, we are all—"

There was a lot of applause at this point. When it died down, Swamiji went on to say, "We are all as close to God as Krishna, or Jesus Christ. We must understand that our energy, instead of going outward, has to come inward to God. And if we can do that simple little thing, which may take many incarnations, we can achieve it too. And that's what the path is all about."

Swamiji's presence and strong words were so energetic and inspiring, the audience again burst into another spontaneous round of applause. The talk show host quickly took a commercial break. They came back and debated more about blind faith and miracles. One man manifested lockets in much the same way that Sai Baba had done, to prove that it's all a hoax. We felt sad for Sai Baba's devotees in the audience. Then the talk show host started in on Sai Baba as a sex offender.

They began talking about sexual abuse from what they termed "God-men." Before we knew it, the talk show host was asking Swamiji about the allegations against him regarding sexual misconduct. She'd seen old articles and knew about the controversy. Swamiji didn't bat an eye, but openly admitted that these things were true. These were his words:

"When I took my vow of sannyas, it was an affirmation. It was difficult for me. I can say that I have come out at the end of the tunnel. I am free in my heart. All these sexual subjects mean absolutely nothing to me, and I thank God for it. I am proud of my life."

The talk show host was stunned and asked in an incredulous voice, "You say the sexual misconduct is true?"

And Swamiji answered, "Absolutely. It was wrong. I can't say it was misconduct. I can say that I did my best, and I finally succeeded."

More commercial breaks and the show concluded in an unremarkable way. They had not succeeded in causing a sensational scene but rather were stunned into silence by truth.

As we were leaving, many people approached Swamiji. Some touched his feet. They all looked at him with great love in their eyes and told him how wonderful it was to hear the truth spoken.

The show aired that night and the ashram residents watched it together. Swamiji was magnificent. The camera angles on him were very good and his voice was clear and strong. There is so much power in truth. As we all came together that evening, it felt as if we became more deeply committed to Master's work and realized the importance of serving this work with someone of such integrity. I knew I would always be at his side, loyal to him, defending him, as Swamiji showed us once again how the truth can set us free.

CHAPTER 7

Medjugorje and Divine Mother

Swamiji said that he always wanted to go to places where the Divine Mother aspect of God is especially manifested. In November 2009 he decided to visit Medjugorje, a little village in Bosnia-Herzegovina, where the Madonna first appeared to six children in 1981 and has been appearing to most of them in the thirty-seven years since then. Through them she gives daily, monthly, and yearly messages to the world. Swamiji wanted this to be a pilgrimage and decided to take only me (his nurse) and Nandini, from Ananda Assisi, as his guides in Medjugorje.

He was not interested in the intellectual or dogmatic aspects of the scene there. Catholics think of Mary as the mother only of Jesus Christ. At Medjugorje, however, the Madonna has repeatedly told the visionaries that all humanity are her children, and that She is above all sectarian differences. Swamiji once wrote: "Before the birth of either Mary or Jesus, was there no Mother? Of course there was! And at Medjugorje, She makes it very clear that *that* is who She really is."

We arrived in Medjugorje after an uneventful flight, but things went slightly awry once we landed on Croatian soil. First, there was not a single restaurant near the airport that would or could serve anything but meat. So, we drove straight through and arrived in Medjugorje around 9 p.m. Nandini had booked very nice rooms at a known guesthouse, but the owner had decided not to have us stay there but instead to put us in his cousin's *pensione*, which was more of a youth hostel. Since he hadn't told Nandini about this in advance, we were unpleasantly surprised. Although the rooms were clean, they were tiny and spartan. The shower in Swamiji's room flooded the bathroom floor and he counted his blessings that it didn't flood the room also! For our late dinner, they prepared large amounts of vegetables for us because we said we were vegetarians. At breakfast the next morning, Swamiji said, "It looks like they took a sledgehammer to the eggs!" Certainly, nice presentation of the food was not happening. The waiter was smoking while serving us! We were surely on another planet.

After we settled Swamiji in his matchbox-size room at 11 p.m., Nandini and I headed off to find our rishi* king a reasonable place to stay. The energy in Medjugorje was quite mixed. The air speaks of the Divine Mother and the clouds are magical, moving, powerful, and full of rain and wind. However, the people who live and work there seemed to be strangely unhappy. They didn't smile, and acted as though they had better things to do than help us. But around midnight we secured a beautiful suite for Swamiji, overlooking the holy mountains. He was quite relieved the next morning when we told him of the new place. After moving into his new room, he stretched out on the bed and slept for about two hours! The proprietors of this new hotel were very service-oriented, and helped Nandini make connections with the seers.

* A Hindu sage or saint.

Nandini was able to connect with Vicka's family. Vicka (pronounced "Vitska") is the oldest visionary and sees the Madonna daily; we hoped Swamiji could meet with her the following day. Nandini also spoke with Mirjana but her family was sick, so we'd only be able to see her at the public satsang. (We weren't sure when that would be—we hoped the following day.) In any case, something was in the air!

Our first few days were strange. As Nandini attempted to obtain interviews for Swamiji with any of the three visionaries then in town, she was told many different stories and promised interviews that didn't happen. We no longer believed anything would happen until it actually did. It seemed that almost everyone was a cousin of one of the visionaries.

After we'd been there for a day and a half, Nandini asked, "Do you perceive anything, Swamiji?" He answered, "No. But that doesn't mean it's not here. Maybe it's only me." Later that day, Swamiji said, "I'm glad I came, but I'm not inspired. So far, anyway."

After many varying messages — "Yes, you have an interview with Mirjana."; "No, it's a public satsang."; "No, it's been canceled due to rain."; . . . — we finally made it to a satsang with Jakov on Tuesday afternoon. (He was ten years old when the visions first came to him and now he was thirty-eight.) A large group of Italian pilgrims was there and he spoke to them fluently in their language. He had a sweet, angelic face that seemed always to be smiling. He spoke for ten minutes or less and then quickly disappeared.

On Wednesday morning we planned to go to Apparition Hill to the "Blue Cross," where the visionaries met secretly during the communist regime. Apparition Hill is the site of the first apparitions in 1981. The Blessed Virgin still appears here to Mirjana on the second of every month. There were many storms and a lot of rain in the days beforehand. We prayed that Wednesday morning would be clear or at least without raining, so that we could somehow get Swamiji up that hill.

Over the years as "Our Lady" has been appearing to the visionaries, She has also been revealing to them "secrets." There are ten secrets, and three of the visionaries have received all ten of them. It is said by the visionaries that once the Madonna has given all ten secrets to the other three visionaries, She will stop appearing. She will then give three warnings to the world. Mirjana will witness the warnings and they will occur on the earth. Some days before each of these warnings, Mirjana will advise a certain priest who will then fast and pray with her for seven days. Then this priest will announce to the world the what, where, and when of the warning about to take place. The prophecy goes on to say that after each warning, people will have time for conversion. And for this reason, the Blessed Virgin calls urgently for conversion and reconciliation. It is said that all who experience conversion and reconciliation must pray and do penance in order to ward off evil and war, and above all to save souls. It is written that, "The ninth and tenth secrets are grave matters. They are the chastisement for the sins of the world. The chastisement can be lessened by prayers and penance, but it cannot be suppressed entirely."

Swamiji was interested in the secrets, as well as in the prophecies of Padre Pio. Padre Pio, a great Italian saint of the last century, predicted that there would descend on our earth three days of darkness. He warned people to stay indoors at that time, because the atmosphere would be dangerously polluted. The visionary children at Garabandal, too, were told by the Virgin Mary that there would be three days of darkness. Swamiji heard a similarly grave prediction made by

Paramhansa Yogananda in church one Sunday when he spoke of the coming depression. He interrupted his talk for a moment to cry loudly, "You don't know what a *terrible cataclysm* is coming!"

It's been thought that perhaps the three days of darkness were connected with the atomic explosions in Hiroshima and Nagasaki, Japan, in 1945. There was a group of Jesuits in Hiroshima as well as a group of Franciscans in Nagasaki who lived at the very center of the explosions; they survived without a scratch and with no aftereffects from the nuclear radiation. Scientists were unable to explain this, but theologians said: "They lived the message of Fatima."

By the grace of Divine Mother and Nandini's immense tenacity, Swamiji was able to be at the apparition on that Wednesday morning and to sit about three feet from the visionary, Mirjana. On account of the rain, the meeting was held in Mirjana's house and not on Apparition Hill. Only a few select people could be inside with Mirjana and the rest of us stood outside surrounding the house. Swamiji couldn't hear much nor did he see that he was so near the visionary. However, he said afterwards, "Although I couldn't hear, I felt a strong love in my heart. This is what matters."

Initially, we felt a certain restraint from the local residents. But when Swamiji donned his nayaswami robes, people began to approach him with reverence, calling him "Padre." Some asked us who he was, and we tried to explain simply. A man in a restaurant approached Swamiji and wanted to share his experiences of Medjugorje. It was very sweet.

We thought our time in Medjugorje had essentially ended with that last apparition gathering after a full day of blessed meetings. However, the next morning brought more adventure and blessings. After three days of rain, wind, and storms, it became clear and sunny. Mirjana gave a public satsang in front of her house. Swamiji was allowed to be inside the gate right in front of her. When she came out, she immediately walked up to him and greeted him. Then she spoke for some time in fluent Italian to the assembled group about her childhood when the apparitions began. She is a dynamic speaker. Nandini asked about the prophesied three days of darkness. Mirjana said that the Madonna had never spoken about this.

Afterwards Swamiji wrote:
I found her extremely clear minded and intelligent—really a joy to listen to. There was quite a bit of emphasis on everyone going to confession, to mass, fasting, and reciting the rosary every day. Catholic stuff, beautiful in its own way, but things that we translate into other terms. Confession, to us, means opening our hearts with complete honesty to God, and to one we really feel can help us. Mass, to us, means *inner* communion. The rosary was beautiful in its way, but I found all that outwardness a little distracting. When people recited, "Pray for us sinners," I substituted the words, "Pray for us, who love You." Why keep on affirming our sinfulness?!

When Mirjana spoke of listening to the priests, she used the word *pastors*, which seemed to me deliberate, and more suitable. I was extremely well impressed with her.

Later that same morning, arrangements were made to have Swamiji transported to the top of Apparition Hill. A very steep path covered with large, jagged rocks leads the pilgrim up to the holy place where "Our Lady" has been seen for these past thirty years. Those

*Swami Kriyananda ("Padre") going up Apparition Hill with
members of the Community of the Last Supper.*

who would brave this climb need sturdy hiking boots and a walking stick. For Swamiji, six young men from the Comunità Cenacolo
("Community of the Last Supper") came with a special chair and
carried him up the hill. These young men are recovering drug addicts
and live in a community that was founded by Sister Elvira. Their tes-
timonies are amazing,+ and through living in spiritual community,
their lives have been completely transformed. These six young men
stopped with Swamiji at each of the Stations of the Cross, allowing
him to pray while they also prayed the rosary. They would continue
to recite the rosary as they climbed farther up the hill. It was one

long and beautiful prayer all the way to the top. When we reached the summit, they requested that Swamiji bless them, and he did so.

After the trip to Apparition Hill, we were taken to the home of Vicka, the oldest and perhaps most dynamic of the visionaries. She sees the Blessed Virgin daily. She hadn't been seeing people for many months—perhaps for three years—owing to great pain she is suffering in her spine. Much of her time seems to be spent in Zagreb (where, incidentally, Swamiji's father was to be transferred from Bucharest, until World War II broke out while the family was visiting the U.S.). We were fortunate to see her at her home on what seems to have been the only day she came back there. I think we were the only ones who were allowed to see her—perhaps in months.

Swamiji felt the visit with Vicka was the highlight of his visit. She spent quite a bit of time with us and was extremely loving. Her husband, Mario, asked Swamiji privately for a blessing. Mario's eyes were full of light and joy, and he spoke for some time about his inner relationship with God. Nandini asked some good questions of Vicka:

Swamiji with Marco, me, Vicka, and Nandini.

1) What does the Madonna say about meditation? "Meditation is very good. First pray. Then read the holy scriptures. After that, be in silence and meditation."

2) What does the Madonna say about other religions? "All religions are the same in the eyes of the Mother. She looks at the heart."

3) What about yoga? "It depends on your heart's intention."

4) How can we overcome the ego? "Live Christ in your heart. Speak less and pray more."

5) How can we better serve others? "By example. If you truly love Christ and serve him through serving others, everyone will be inspired."

Swamiji asked Vicka if she would ask the Divine Mother for him whether there was anything more he could do for Her in this life. He told her that he'd been serving Her for over sixty-one years, and had done nearly everything he could think of in this service. Vicka promised to ask that question. Swamiji said that he had no outward answer from her, but upon returning from Medjugorje he felt Divine Mother's answer: "Love me ever more deeply, in your heart."

It's hard to express in words what it was like to be in the presence of Swamiji and Vicka. We were moved to tears watching them talk, and even while taking photos of them together. Long after returning home, Swamiji would weep when he spoke of Vicka, and say that he felt she was a dear friend.

He said also that since his visit to Medjugorje he had felt so much bliss in his heart he could hardly bear it!

CHAPTER 8

Circumstances Are Neutral

Early in 2008, Swamiji decided it was time to move the work in India to Pune. He felt Ananda India needed to start a community where devotees could live together. So the search was on to find land outside of Pune where we could begin to build a community. Since Swamiji was ready to move to Pune immediately, the scouts were looking not only for land but also for housing in the city where we could live right away. There would be many obstacles to overcome and much tapasya to perform before the community would manifest.

In the summer of 2008 Swamiji had a speaking tour in Los Angeles. As many know, Swamiji had been dismissed from his guru's organization, Self-Realization Fellowship (SRF), in 1962, and he struggled for the rest of his life for reconciliation with the organization. The separation was a great source of sadness to him. On a personal level, he saw them as his gurubhais, and treasured the time they'd shared together serving Master. On a broader level, he felt that harmony between the organizations would please Master and would strengthen both organizations in their service. Till this day, however, that reconciliation has not taken place.

During the Los Angeles tour, it was arranged for Swamiji to meet with three SRF monks. At the SRF Lake Shrine Swamiji met for over an hour with monks who had joined SRF many years after Master's passing: Vishwananda, Chidananda (now the president), and another brahmachari. Jyotish and Devi Novak, the spiritual directors of Ananda worldwide, and Krishnadas and Mantradevi LoCicero, the spiritual directors of Ananda Los Angeles, joined Swamiji for this meeting. A large group of Ananda devotees were also at the Lake Shrine, walking the grounds and meditating, sending Swamiji love and light. It was a very disheartening experience for Swamiji; while he had hoped to create a bridge, they just wanted to tell him what a bad person he was and to call him on the carpet about a variety of strange things. He said afterwards that they were so self-righteous the idea of reconciliation seemed impossible.

The 1962 ouster from SRF and the continuing schism between SRF and Ananda had surely been the greatest tests in Swamiji's life. After meeting the SRF monks, he had some unusual episodes of profound weakness and dizziness. He was unable even to eat that evening and had to lie down on the couch at Krishnadas and Mantradevi's house. The following morning, he couldn't get out of bed and slept until lunchtime. His vital signs and blood tests were normal so he continued with all of the planned events of the weekend.

Usually when returning home after such a big weekend, Swamiji would need to rest for a few days and then he would bounce back to full energy. It had been a week since we returned to the Village and each day brought no notable improvement. We'd been trying to walk with him a few times a day, but it tired him so much it was a cause for concern.

Dr. Peter Van Houten felt we should check things out by having Swamiji undergo a Treadmill ECG. Swamiji passed his treadmill test with flying colors! In fact, his heart pumped more effectively with exercise than when he was at rest.

His cardiologist gave the go-ahead to start a consistent exercise program. Swamiji reluctantly agreed to an exercise regime of walking in his gardens at Crystal Hermitage as well as doing the Energization Exercises every day. Due to profound fatigue, he had not done the Energization Exercises in a while. We planned that Swamiji would walk in the gardens three to four times a day and enlisted the help of others to come and walk with him. I did the morning round with him; Jyotish and Devi came for the late afternoon walk and then would stay with him for tea; others helped with walks in between.

One morning early into the new regime, as he and I were walking around the garden, he had to stop and rest in the gazebo. As he sat, he spoke about giving up the body; he felt he had done enough and was finished with this lifetime. He said he didn't really need to write Part Two of *The Promise of Immortality* because he'd already written most of the information in *Rays of the One Light*. At this point, I very quietly asked, "Swamiji, what about the work in India?" He took a deep breath and said, "Yes, I know. I'm needed there." I'd been talking to him earlier that week about how we could get him in shape if he wanted to tour the major cities in India. And there was the building of the community in Pune to consider. At the end of this conversation, he looked at me quite sternly and said, "Let's see if we can make this happen." From that moment on, he moved beyond simply accepting the situation with SRF, and began truly to glorify it. He actually did the tour of India during the last eight months of his life, about three and a half years later.

The following week he led an amazing Spiritual Renewal Week. Dharmadas and Nirmala Schuppe, then spiritual directors of Ananda India, attended and talked with Swamiji about the next steps for Ananda India. This seemed to help him immensely. His enthusiasm for the work in India returned full force. Swamiji was his old self again, full of joy, energy, and enthusiasm, talking more and more about his return to India. He began sharing his plans to move to Pune soon after Christmas and hoped to have a large celebration for Master's birthday, which he thought would be a wonderful way to launch the work there. Only ten days earlier, he had asked me in a very grave and tired voice if I thought he would ever return to India. I told him most emphatically, "Yes, I do."

Swamiji's battle with profound fatigue lasted until the end of his life. His despondency about his relationship with SRF also continued. But all of this was simply the physical plane. His soul soared in bliss, ready to engage in hand-to-hand combat with Satan when needed, as he moved forward to serve his guru's work.

Swamiji had been wondering about options for housing in Pune and was open to almost anything. Amol Parkhi, a devotee from Pune, suggested we could all rent a section of one of the newer apartment complexes. Swamiji could have his own apartment and the rest of us could live in adjacent units. Swamiji liked this idea, since it might encourage some Pune devotees also to move into the complex, helping to launch a sense of community. We could have room for the Sangha offices, Kriya ministry, and publications, as well as a temple for daily meditations, satsangs, and more.

Between the months of September and December 2008, a scouting crew found a new apartment complex in the part of Pune closest to the land where we hoped to build our community. Deposits were

Swami Kriyananda holding a fire ceremony in Pune.

made, rent paid, and work begun to make the apartments ready for Swamiji and all of us.

Immediately after Christmas, we began packing the belongings in Guru Kripa, Swamiji's home in Gurgaon, for our move to Pune. Somehow, we got everything packed in time; Swamiji took off for a short vacation in Goa while many of us went to Pune to get the apartments ready for his arrival. He moved into his apartment in January 2009 and during his time there accomplished some import-ant projects. He completed editing Catherine Kairavi's book, *Two Souls, Four Lives.* He rewrote his autobiography, *The Path*, renaming it *The New Path*, and recorded himself reading the new book aloud.

Swamiji's primary goal, however, continued to be getting the community started in Pune. Miraculously, land was purchased and building commenced. In January 2010, Swamiji's home in our Ananda India community near Pune was declared "ready!" I have to say, this was quite an overstatement!

Biraj Palmer, who was supervising much of the construction work on the Pune land, wrote about Swamiji's house just a week before he was scheduled to move in:

There have been one hundred people, each day, working on the building site over the past two weeks! All the window arches and final painting are getting completed today; on Tuesday, there is a big workday with our Pune congregation to do deep cleaning; the bubble-wrapped furniture comes by truck Tuesday night; the glass windows get installed Wednesday night; and the last electrical and plumbing hookups happen Thursday — if all goes well. . . . It's a race, but Vidura assures me that 'we have a good chance' of winning!

Bless you all. Keep your prayers and blessings coming for a successful finish to this fun and fascinating adventure. As Narayani put it, "Divine Mother has to be in this flow. Because it's not possible that humans by themselves could build seven buildings in only seven months!"

Swamiji was in Goa waiting for the construction to be finished so he could move in. But he was having a difficult time with the body again and wrote me the following email from Goa:

Dear Miriam:

I've been getting a good rest. I must have been very tired, because for the first two weeks I spent most of my time sleeping in my room. Yesterday, finally, I felt refreshed and rested. But today again I am tired. My heart is tired. And I've begun to wonder: Is India good for me? I hope

I'll be fine at Watunde [the town where our community is located]. Remember all the troubles I had in my first years here. Remember how I left India last May, on the point of dying. Your memory will tell you better than mine how I was during the interim period.

I'd appreciate your thoughts. We've had a lot of salt in our diet, and that may be contributing to my heart's fatigue. I'm happy to live usefully, wherever Master wants me. But I'd certainly find it easier to serve if my heart were only not so tired all the time.

Maybe I'll be fine again tomorrow. Meanwhile, however, you might give all this a little thought.

love,
Swami

Swami Kriyananda always had time for everyone.

I responded:

Dear Swamiji,

The illnesses and diseases that have often manifested in your body, although they seem physical in nature and we treat you with various medical interventions, I've always seen as completely spiritual in their causation. Just as the Christ underwent crucifixion, it wasn't about him needing to undergo such intense physical suffering, but was rather for the mitigation of his disciples' karma and also somewhat for the redemption of the mass karma incurred during Kali Yuga.

In these past years, I've seen you go through many passions of Christ. However, last May was a much deeper Passion, ending with a profound Resurrection. You were dying, Swamiji, and there was no way you would have survived all the critical conditions that were present in your body except through divine intervention. You told me afterwards it was Master's *will*, as opposed to his grace, that you survived, and you felt now you'd live a lot longer. As you came quite suddenly out of this critical situation with the body, you told Asha you realized it had been Satan trying to prevent you from bringing forth this new renunciate order. One can only imagine how deep and universally significant the consequences will be from the launching of this new swami order, and most especially in India.

Swamiji, if it seems that India is not good for you, it's surely because there is still yet a great work to be done there. And perhaps much of the tapasya needed for such a work will be done in your poor body. I'm sorry if this is true, because it's been wonderful to see you so full of good health and vitality since last June. Let's wait and see how you do after you get home. With Lila's cooking, Jyotish and Devi coming, filming to start, and countless devotees eagerly awaiting your darshan, you will, without a doubt, be given the strength to finish this great work Master has given to you.

You're ever in my prayers.

love,
Miriam

Moving Swamiji into his new house in the Pune community was quite a project. Nirmala and others were successful in making him comfortable in his new house. Even though Swamiji's house was declared "finished," Dharmadas can attest that the house was far from it! It required constant repairs to keep electricity, lights, computer, and hot water functioning.

Most of the staff dwellings were still mere shells, so it was difficult to find places for Swamiji's staff to stay. The houses for staff were small "kutirs": one-room studios with a bathroom and a small area for a combined bedroom and meditation area. At this point in their construction, there were no windows, no screens, no electricity, no water, no kitchen! The Schuppes' house was the farthest along, but it was still under construction. However, Nirmala invited all three of us, Lila, Lakshman, and myself, to camp out in their house.

Because of her service as Swamiji's cook, Lila had no choice except to completely move onto the land into whatever quarters she could find. For a long time, she stayed in what would eventually become Dharmadas's office. Lila's first night in the house was pitch dark with no electricity, candles, or flashlight! Lakshman's service as Swamiji's secretary required constant electricity and internet, so he needed to live in the Pune apartments and come out to the land when he could find a ride. I was offered a space on the floor in the Schuppes' living room, but I felt there was no way I could stay there camping out, so I went back to the Pune apartments. Not very yogic, but there you have it.

Later that same night, Swamiji phoned around midnight. I knew that eating so much salty food during his long vacation in Goa was putting him into congestive heart failure. Dharmadas and I, by phone, had been making almost daily adjustments to his diuretics to try to prevent this from happening. But it had been difficult to do this effectively long distance. I thought for this one night he would be okay until morning, when I would dose him quite heavily with diuretics. But that proved not the case. In the middle of the night he became very short of breath and feared he was having a heart attack. He even tried to phone Dr. Peter in the U.S. before he called me, because he knew I wasn't physically available (the apartments were an hour's drive from the land). There wasn't anything that could be done in the night, so Swamiji agreed to wait until morning.

The next morning, after the dose of diuretics, Swamiji began to feel somewhat better, and soon recovered completely. It was obvious, however, that I needed to move to the land and spend many of my nights there. I had hoped I could commute to the land sometimes from our apartments in Pune, but that just wasn't working out. I decided to move to the land just as Lila had done. In fact, as I was looking at Lila that day, I saw how clear her face had become. Such joyful blue eyes. I saw what it meant to completely surrender one's preferences, and I was inspired to try and do it myself.

In these first days there was no running water—certainly no purified water—minimal electricity; no furniture; no glass on many of the windows, with bugs and mosquitoes freely coming in; and workers (sometimes as pesky as mosquitoes) coming in and out all day. But soon we had purified water in the Schuppes' kitchen, more electricity (it was usually off from 2 p.m. to 6 p.m. and off again from 11 p.m. to 8 a.m.), and there was running water in the bathroom. Progress was happening!!!

With every step, I had to face full on many of my ego-gratifying desires. I wanted running water—it didn't have to be hot; cold showers are fine (there was no hot water). I wanted pure water to drink, and this didn't seem to me to be optional. Some electricity seemed like a good thing. However, what I found was that I literally had to give up every single desire (bottled water could be obtained, but you had to work for it!).

One of the hardest things for me is to live in dirt. Swamiji used to tell of seeing a young beggar girl outside a temple in Puri. By the way she looked around her with dismay, he sensed that she had been royalty in her last life and through greed had been reduced to this low state. I wondered if something similar had happened to me, because I can't stand to be dirty, especially to have dirty hands or feet. I can't even look at the poor people in hovels along the roadsides. Yet, now I found myself sleeping on a very dirty floor, with everything I owned getting increasingly covered in red clay dirt, and no way to correct the situation. Mice ran around my bed on the floor and chewed their way through plastic bags to get at whatever was inside them! What little running water we'd finally gotten was gone in an instant one morning when a broken pipe under the sink suddenly flooded the kitchen floor.

I tried to surrender and accept all these really quite small hardships, which still seemed so big to the ego. If, at each point of resistance, I prayed from Master's book, *Whispers from Eternity*:

> O Spirit, I care not if all sufferings come to me, or all things be taken away from me; I pray only that my love for Thee never fade through my own negligence. May my love for Thee burn brightly forever on the altar of my constant remembrance.

. . . I would move through the resistance, and there was God! The bliss was so intense at times I'd weep off and on most of the day. One morning I came up against yet another point of resistance. I was almost ready to give up and tell Swamiji that I had failed in my efforts to live on the land and I would have to move back to the city apartment. But it took only a few minutes of not giving in to the ego, to feel Master's grace. Something let go inside of me again, and it was another day filled with an intense bliss.

Swamiji was happily puttering around in his new house, focused deeply on writing his new movie about Master's life (*The Answer*). He managed to overlook the inconveniences of his new house and seemed quite content.

During this time I had my 56th birthday, and it was a tremendous day, full of very difficult physical challenges: no electricity, kitchen flooding, and no running water anywhere. There was no functioning toilet, there was no way to make hot water for a cup of tea, no shower, and so much dirt, so much noise, and a constant barrage of workers in the house (mostly in the living room of the Schuppes', my bedroom!). Yet . . . this gift of bliss.

It felt as though we were all with Swamiji watching a great movie. I so hoped someone would make popcorn and lemonade! Then, out of the blue, Swamiji announced he wanted us to take a break and go to the new Westin Hotel in Pune! Lila and I were thrilled through and through. Enough of the bliss!!!! We really needed to take a shower and wash our hair! Not to mention washing some socks!! Mamma mia!

The Westin Hotel is a beautiful five-star, and at that time brand-new, hotel in Pune. We were stunned by full-wall water features and visual delights at every turn. We had dinner that evening in their lovely Italian restaurant, and the food was indescribable. The next morning, we all gathered in their breakfast buffet dining room. This room had almost floor-to-ceiling windows on one side that looked out onto beautifully landscaped gardens. But the most stunning visuals in this room were the overhead light fixtures. These were designed to depict waves of the sea, with clear glass and aquamarine glass combined in a wavelike design. I found myself sitting at our large round table alone with Swamiji. We were facing each other, and I was looking up over his head, mesmerized by these beautiful aquamarine light fixtures. The thought came into my mind how incredible it was to be one minute in such a dirty and challenging setting, and the very next to be in such an elegant and astral environment. I heard Swamiji's deep throaty chuckle and I lowered my eyes to look at him. With a twinkle in his blue eyes, he softly said, "It's all a dream."

CHAPTER 9

Suffering Is Needed to Find God

During a TV interview, Swamiji was asked, "Do we have to suffer in order to find God?" I was a little startled at how quickly he responded: "Oh, yes." He went on to explain that there are two essential conditions for knowing God. One is the willingness to face any test that comes to us and accept it with love and courage. Swamiji then said that many Christians believe that holiness is demonstrated by the intensity of one's suffering. But the true teaching of Christ, and the second essential condition, is to maintain a serene attitude in the face of suffering. Swamiji demonstrated his inner freedom time and time again by accepting everything as coming from the Guru, and therefore embracing it wholeheartedly.

Swamiji had returned to New Delhi in August of 2007, and by December of that year, he hadn't been feeling well for over four months. We decided we needed to rule out certain possibilities. First, we arranged for him to have an ultrasound of his gallbladder and, indeed, gallstones were found. Before doing surgery on the gallbladder, the gastroenterologist felt a need to rule out any other abnormalities.

So Swamiji was scheduled for a colonoscopy at the Max Saket Hospital, a beautiful and modern facility in New Delhi.

Swamiji's gastroenterologist, Dr. Tandon, a lovely older gentleman, was performing the procedure. It seemed to be taking an unusually long time, so I went to see what was going on. Dr. Tandon showed me films of what he had found, and said there appeared to be a tumor. Because of its size and location, it was probably malignant and metastatic. Swamiji was lying on the table in the same room, but because he didn't have in his hearing aids, he didn't know what the doctor had said. When I turned to him, he demanded to know what was happening. I bent down so I could speak into his good ear and said, "Swamiji, it looks like you have colon cancer, and it is most likely malignant and metastatic." This might seem a bit abrupt, but Swamiji always wanted the truth. He gave a slight shudder and then became quiet and inward.

The doctor wanted to do a CT scan immediately to see if there were metastases. Swamiji had to wait two hours for the scan in a somewhat darkened room; he seemed to appreciate the darkness and remained inward. I felt strongly that we needed to let many people know so prayers could be started. Nirmala, however, felt we should wait until we knew more instead of causing people to panic. I felt a strong need for prayers but didn't want to go against Nirmala's wishes. I decided to call two of my closest friends. One of them was Shivani Lucki in Italy, and I knew she would move heaven and earth to get the prayers going. When I called her and told her what was happening, she quickly said, "I'm on it." I then called my other dear friend, Narayani Anaya, in Spain. I knew she had been through a similar experience with cancer. Her response was startling in its power. She said very firmly, "These things can be changed." I was standing on the sidewalk outside the hospital, and I felt her words root me strongly into the flow of Master's grace. Due to the time zone difference and things moving so fast, I couldn't let Ananda America know anything just yet. The doctors were almost positive there would be extensive metastases, but perhaps they didn't understand the power of prayer!

After Swamiji's CT scan, Dr. Tandon came out of the imaging room shaking his head. He said, "I can't believe it. There are no metastases." He folded his hands in pronam and Nirmala placed her hands around his and wept. Swamiji still almost certainly had cancer, but at least there were no metastases. We now had to wait for the biopsy to learn for sure whether it was malignant.

Swamiji had a day of waiting to find out the results of the biopsy. The report wasn't easy to accept, as it came back malignant. But even with this diagnosis, miracles continued to unfold. The team of surgeons at the Max Hospital in Saket was assembled, and as we met each doctor it was clear they were some of India's finest. Not only were they competent physicians, they were kind, respectful, and loving towards Swamiji and all of us.

We had been told that Swamiji would have to be in ICU for at least three days postoperatively, and that visiting hours there would be severely limited. On the day of admission to the hospital for pre-op preparations, a miracle came through our dear friend, Sri Kaarthikeyan, the former Director of India's Central Bureau of Investigation (similar to the FBI in the U.S.). Sri Kaarthikeyanji, who is on the Board of Internal Medicine for Max Hospital, wrote an email to his good friend, the owner and chief cardiologist of Max. He kindly asked that Swamiji's nurse be allowed to be with him in the ICU.

We also had the added blessing of Hriman and Padma McGilloway, the spiritual directors of Ananda Washington, who had come for a visit and were now part of Swamiji's medical team! Hriman played the important role of guarding Swamiji's hospital room door. At all hours of the day and night, and especially in the very early morning hours, there's someone wanting to enter the hospital room for a trivial reason like delivering a newspaper or a "delicious" powdered Nescafe coffee! Hriman stationed himself outside the door to prevent anyone coming in unless they had a good reason to do so. Padma's presence was also invaluable as will be told later in the story — stay tuned! We were also allowed to "keep" Swamiji's hospital room even though he would be in ICU for some days. This meant Dharmadas, Nirmala, and I had a place to sleep and stay during those days.

On the day of surgery, Swamiji woke up around 2 a.m. and told us he was "swimming in bliss." All that morning, Swamiji's bliss was palpable, filling his room and all of us. He wrote the following message:

Dear Everyone:

Today is the big day. I feel no fear, only bliss.

In my heart there is only love for everyone, *without exception*; no hurts; only deep gratitude.

My will for everyone on earth is PEACE, LOVE, BLISS, and FREEDOM.

Swami Kriyananda

It's impossible to describe the presence of Divine Power at this time, as all the prayer vigils started. One could say there was a deep sense of not being alone, but it was so much more than that. It was a glimpse of knowing that we are "a part of all that is."

Later that morning, the surgical team came to take Swamiji to the operating theater. We were all allowed to accompany Swamiji as they wheeled his stretcher onto the service elevator. We followed him and his stretcher down some long halls until we finally reached the huge swinging double doors that were the entrance to the operating suites. We were not allowed to go beyond this point. We all crushed together, however, to peer through the small windows in those large swinging doors to catch a last glimpse of Swamiji.

Once he was through the doors, they took a left turn down another hall. Swamiji craned his neck and looked back over his left shoulder to take one last look at all of us watching him. And suddenly from under the sheets, up shot his right arm, giving us the sweetest wave goodbye. If you've ever seen Swamiji wave, you know that his hand moves in such a way as to be saying "Yes!" No matter what was happening in his outer circumstances, Swamiji was saying "Yes to life!"

Swamiji's surgery was considered high risk. The physicians expressed concern about the length of time he would be under general anesthesia, as well as about unforeseen complications during surgery. Immediately after surgery, Swamiji was taken to the intensive care unit. As he transitioned from general anesthesia to IV pain management, he was in a lot of pain. When I saw him for the first time after surgery, he was clearly in pain, and said an interesting thing. As I tried to reassure him that the pain would be relieved soon and the doctors wanted him to sleep, he said, "I don't want to sleep, I want comfort." I knew the one person who could give Swamiji comfort in this moment. I quickly went to find Nirmala and she went in to work her magic of comfort and loving presence. She was able to calm and comfort him, so that his body could relax and the pain medicine could work. When I saw him a short time later, he was much improved. At this time, he was puffy and not really able to move his body, since he was "guarding" the abdomen to prevent pain.

This is where the next miracle comes in. Actually, two miracles unfolded. One was that I *was* allowed to stay in the ICU, and the other was how quickly Swamiji's post-op condition changed. I stayed with him for a few hours and then, since he was sleeping, I went to the room to sleep a little too. When I returned in about an hour and a half, Swamiji looked amazingly well. The puffiness was gone, and he had good color. He was relatively free of pain and was awake and alert. He could also turn himself in bed easily and was doing so!

I had had many concerns about this first night in ICU, as the recovery from such extensive surgery can be difficult. But here I found Swamiji clearly "swimming in bliss." For the next several hours, every time Swamiji woke up, he would tell stories of his friendship with Master. On the morning of the surgery, he had started to write an article on friendship and especially what it means to be in a divine friendship with Master. Swamiji told a story of once laughing so hard with Master that tears were running down their cheeks. He talked about the depth of love that Master has for all of us in saying he will return again and again, a trillion lifetimes if necessary, to redeem us. Standing at Swamiji's bedside listening to his stories of Master's love for us, I felt Master very much in the room, standing with his arm around my shoulders, also enjoying Swamiji's stories.

It was an amazing night, and the next day Swamiji was out of bed, sitting in a chair for some hours and reading an e-book. He would say over and over, "Please tell everyone I appreciate all the prayers, and I can feel everyone's presence with me."

Still, Swamiji's body was not yet stabilized and he had to stay in the ICU for a total of four days. Because of the blood thinners he took, there was some internal bleeding that caused severe anemia. This required blood transfusions. Swamiji very much preferred to have the blood of a devotee rather than an anonymous donor. So, I enlisted Lakshman Heubert, Swamiji's secretary, to rally all of the devotees at the ashram to get their blood type checked and to see if their hematocrits were high enough to give blood. In the meantime, Padma went with me to the blood bank to inform them that we were working on getting our own blood donors. The supervisor there was a somewhat fierce woman. When we came breezing in to tell her we were going to use other donors, she became quite indignant, asking in a very snooty voice, "So, our blood isn't good enough for your swami?" She said the word "swami" with a sneer. I was dumbfounded—I had no clue how to respond to her anger. I hadn't slept very much in the last two weeks and all I knew was that our Swamiji needed blood, he wanted devotee blood, and we needed it ASAP. I stood there stunned and speechless. But Padma knew exactly how to handle the situation. In a most loving voice, she said, "Don't you know, it's such a deep blessing to be able to give one's blood to one's guru?" The supervisor melted. Now she understood.

As good fortune would have it, I was the same blood type as Swamiji and was able to give blood immediately. Priya McDivitt (Wong), who at the time was working on establishing a Living Wisdom school in Gurgaon, was also able to give blood that day. The next day he received a third unit donated by one of our dear Indian devotees, Mickey Dutt. Such a blessing to give your own blood to your beloved teacher!

By now, Swamiji had come out of the intensive care unit and was in his hospital suite. It was a perfect setup, in that Swamiji had his own room with an extra bed where Dharmadas could sleep, and there was an adjoining room with two pullout sofas where Nirmala and I could stay. Swamiji's room had a full bathroom, and ours a half bath and a small kitchenette. The Indian culture really knows how to take care of patients and their families!

Swamiji continued to recover and was finally allowed to go home. He'd arranged ahead of time to have two of our members waiting to meet him when he arrived: Mr. Bij, whom Swamiji had initiated into Kriya back in 1959, and Ved Sharma, another close member. Swamiji chatted with all of us, and several times during the conversation, he said, "I am so blissful."

He wrote the following words that same day:

Bliss! Ah, what bliss. I returned this afternoon from the hospital after spending a week there. Why speak of the hardships? The experience was perfectly heavenly.

I went into surgery with bliss. I came out with more bliss. Was there pain? Well, of course there was, but I've always said a little pain never hurt anybody. I simply chose, as I always do, to think about something more interesting. (There's so much else in life to hold one's attention.)

I was *deeply* touched to receive your many messages of love, prayer, and support. I think in some ways that is what this week meant most of all to me. I've been hurt and betrayed so often in my life that my reaction to it has been simply not to think what other people's opinions are about me. My job, simply, as I've seen it, has been to love *them*.

"Only the good
that is gleaned
from an experience
should be allowed into
the reservoir of memory"
—Paramhansa Yogananda

Swami Kriyananda was often in bliss.

Moreover, I've never really cared to think of myself as anyone important. My goal is to get out of the ego. I've simply tried, therefore, to serve Master, and his presence in all of you, to the best of my ability. I was moved, then, to receive such an outpouring of love from you all. Thank you, humbly, in his name, and from my heart.

When I wrote before going into surgery, that I loved (as indeed I do love) everyone *without exception,* of course I thought of the various people about whom I might have felt some hesitation to make such a statement—people who have hurt me, betrayed me, tried to destroy me. I didn't want to say such a thing unless I could say it sincerely. But there simply were no exceptions. There aren't now, either. Everyone is trying, each in his or her own way, to attain Divine Bliss. This is, I have found, the reason why we should love *everyone*—not personally, but impersonally (that is to say, wanting nothing for ourselves), in God. I've come out of major double surgery feeling more full of love than ever.

The personnel at the hospital were *wonderful*. The nurses are angels. And the doctors — all I can say is, I've seldom seen such beauty and nobility in so many men's faces in one place together as in the doctors there.

The Bhagavad Gita, Chapter 5, verses 20 and 21, states, "Such sages [who view everything even-mindedly], established in the one Supreme Being and unwavering in their discrimination, are neither jubilant when confronted by pleasant experiences nor depressed when confronted by painful ones. / Feeling no attraction to the sensory world (either subtle or gross), the yogi lives in the ever-new joy of his own being. United to Spirit, he attains the perfection of Absolute Bliss.

I am no sage, and have yet far to go on the path, but I have to say that those words describe my own experience as I went into surgery. When my heart was operated on thirteen years ago, I went into the operation with a joyful attitude, but this time something more happened. It wasn't attitude. I did have a joyful, accepting attitude, but what emerged *from within* this time, was much more: It was bliss.

One might theorize that, according to those stanzas of the Gita, one ought to be equally joyful in going out to a good restaurant for a delicious dinner and being carted off to the hospital to have his guts ripped out. The contrast is ludicrous. But that is *exactly how I felt*. In a way, indeed, the guts ripping part was even better, for it resulted in some (I hope) permanent gain within me. It was simply *wonderful*. And your prayers helped make it so. Again, thank you.

~ ~ ~ ~ ~ ~ ~ ~ ~ ~

Swamiji tolerated the first round of chemotherapy well. However, the second round, given two weeks later, caused profound diarrhea, with resulting exhaustion and dehydration. These symptoms were exacerbated by some previous post-op complications. Swamiji's trip to Italy had to be postponed for some days as a result, after which he was well enough to make the flight back to Italy.

Swamiji was very happy to be back in his little house in Ananda Assisi and in semi-seclusion. He remained weakened from the surgery and chemotherapy, and kept saying that his heart was very tired. We made arrangements for him to be seen locally by an oncologist who would manage the subsequent rounds of chemotherapy. This man stated that in light of Swamiji's age and health, he didn't think Swamiji needed such strong doses of chemo, if, in fact, he needed them at all. This gave Swamiji outward confirmation of guidance he'd doubtless already been feeling inwardly: to stop the chemotherapy entirely, prioritizing quality of life over possibly prolonging it. Swamiji said that his life was in God's hands, and that He had protected him many times in this life.

Swamiji felt that the coming year promised to be one of his most important. He wanted to have the energy to do all the things that were planned. He had Master's mahasamadhi celebration in India, launching *Revelations of Christ* in April in Italy, and, in the U.S., the fortieth anniversary of Ananda along with his sixtieth anniversary of discipleship. If he were to continue the chemotherapy as originally planned through the first of April, with the following six months for recovery, the year would be pretty much gone. Swamiji said again and again in those days that Divine Mother had always taken care of him, and would continue to do so.

CHAPTER 10

Seville and a Soulmate

In 2003 Narayani Anaya came to Assisi from her home in Spain to meet Swamiji for the first time. She was immediately aware of a profound connection with him and a reverence for one she came to think of as "her king." She was unencumbered at that time in her life, and had some resources, so she began to follow Swamiji as he traveled to the various Ananda communities around the world. She would come to Assisi, for example, and do seva there. Next she would meet him in India and find a way to stay in the ashram and serve. Wherever she went, her focus was Swamiji and service to his work. She continued in this way for the next few years.

I was immediately attracted to her spiritual depth and great devotion to Swamiji, so I always encouraged her to follow him. At one point I thought I should check my intuition; I mentioned to Swamiji that Narayani was thinking to follow him to Los Angeles that summer. With a warm smile and great sweetness, Swamiji said, "Oh, wonderful! I'd love to have her there. Some people are so dear, you want to have them near."

In early 2010, Swamiji asked Narayani to plan a trip for him to Seville, Spain. Paramhansa Yogananda had said publicly that in a former incarnation he had been William the Conqueror. He'd also said that he had been a king in Spain who drove out the Moors. Swamiji felt that Yogananda had been King Ferdinand III, known as El Santo (the Saint), and that he himself had been his son Alfonso X. Ferdinand III was only eighteen when he became king of Castile, a kingdom torn apart by numerous raids led by both Christians and Moors, as well as by internal rebellions. He was one of history's most gifted and formidable warriors, and was able to unite permanently the kingdoms of León and Castile, expelling the Muslims from Andalusia and conquering more Islamic territory than any other Christian. King Ferdinand's legacy is far-reaching and enduring; he is considered one of the greatest monarchs who ever ruled. While King Ferdinand III succeeded in driving the Moors out of Spain, his son Alfonso X (The Wise) united as Christians the many smaller kingdoms that existed in Spain.

Ferdinand III's body is enshrined in a chapel in Seville, in a casket of gold and crystal at the foot of a statue of the Virgin. He is the only king whose earthly crown has never been taken away and still encircles his head, proof of the enormous regard of his people. Much more importantly, his body is incorrupt, proof of his purity and sainthood. Ferdinand's tomb is opened to the public one day each year, usually on May 30.

Swamiji made plans to travel to Seville in May of 2010 to visit the tomb. He also wanted to offer a lecture to launch the newly completed Spanish edition of *Autobiography of a Yogi*. Narayani and the devotees in Spain planned a beautiful trip for Swamiji. Swamiji wanted only Narayani, Narya and Laura Tosetto, and me to accom-

With Narayani in Seville.

pany him. Others from Ananda Assisi and Spain stayed in other ho-
tels nearby, but he asked for privacy and seclusion during the days
when he planned to view the incorrupt body of King Ferdinand III.

I wrote a letter at the time to Asha, saying:

Swamiji becomes more and more transparent? clarified?
What word to use to describe such a divine occurrence? His
perfection, that divine perfection he's attained, is so beloved
to be around. And what a blessing to be with him so much!

Something profound happened in Seville. Swamiji's back gave
him intense pain the entire time. He called Narya, Narayani, or me
to him at least every two hours, sometimes every ten minutes, night

Swamiji with Narya, Laura, and Narayani in Seville.

and day, to give massages and try to lessen the unrelenting distress. The three of us, and especially Swamiji, had very little sleep. Somewhere in the midst of all this care, Swamiji discovered Narayani to be a true and dear friend.

Narya and Laura were his protectors, and it was a joy to watch them — they were so lovely with him. Narya is like a dear, sweet father to him and was utterly attentive to Swamiji's needs. Laura's command of Spanish was invaluable. They were both completely selfless in their service to him. I loved traveling with them. As we moved Swamiji from airport to airport, hotel to hotel, or event to event I felt he was perfectly safe in their care.

It was an incredibly inspiring trip, but Swamiji had many obstacles to overcome in order to go, including high blood sugars, severe pain in his upper spine, and a canceled flight in Milan causing hours of delay. Also, at the last minute, the city of Seville changed the day from May 30 to May 28, so Swamiji had to leave earlier than planned. However, thanks to the many prayers offered, Swamiji arrived safely in Seville, a place he said felt like home.

Narayani had arranged for Swamiji to stay in an old and majestic hotel, very much a palace for our rishi king. From the hotel he could see the cathedral where the body of Ferdinand III rests, as well as the Palacio Andaluz, the home of Ferdinand when he lived in Seville (1199–1252 AD).

With thoughtful planning on Narayani's part and the right connections, Swamiji was allowed to spend an hour alone in the chapel with the body of Ferdinand after the crowds had filed through. There were still a few tourists coming in and out, but it was much more quiet and private, and a special gift for Swamiji.

Though he had begun the day with tremendous pain in his back and had required a wheelchair, Swamiji stood up and walked into the chapel. He stepped up on the podium and stood in front of Ferdinand's body for forty minutes. He placed his hands gently on the altar and remained unmoving, seemingly not breathing, for those forty minutes. There was a feeling of immense power in this chapel. Great waves of vibration seemed to come from the body of Ferdinand. Swamiji remained meditative for some time after leaving the chapel and did not make any comments about his experience—not until years afterward.

Swamiji eventually told us that he had felt for some time that Narayani was to take a more active role in his life, but he did not want to be mistaken about this. He stood in front of the incorrupt body of Ferdinand III communing with Master about this question, until he felt in his heart the answer: Narayani was, indeed, supposed to be at his side for the remaining three and half years of his life.

At Swamiji's request, Narayani became his "personal trainer." It was deeply moving to see them together, especially in moments when they didn't know someone was there. One day I came upon them walking along his driveway in Assisi, slowly, arm in arm, heads bent toward one another, talking lovingly of Master. When he saw me, he invited me to join them so he could use my arm to lean on also. Now, he was walking four times a day and doing his Energization Exercises again. He would get tired, but he was becoming stronger every day.

Master said very little on the topic of soul mates. Swamiji remembered Master quoting Sri Yukteswar saying to Yogananda, "until our twin souls merge in the Infinite." Swamiji wondered if Yogananda and Sri Yukteswar were soul mates. Swamiji told us Master had said "it was necessary to meet one's soul mate before merging in final liberation, into the Infinite."

On more than a few occasions, Swamiji mentioned that he felt Narayani was his soul mate and that it was important that he meet her once again. Somehow, her presence was crucial to his attaining final liberation in this lifetime. From what little he said, I couldn't tell if he completely understood it himself. But clearly her presence was an important blessing for him, right up to the moment of his passing. (This will be described in the final chapter.)

CHAPTER 11

Transformative Power

"As many as received him, to them gave he
power to become the sons of God."

Here are some special memories of experiences of the spiritual power flowing through Swamiji:

In the fall of 2009, Nandini arranged for Anima, an Italian TV station, to make several DVDs of Swamiji. He was able to do in three days what the filmmakers had thought would take at least seven. While filming in the town of Assisi, a few retakes were needed because of a motorcycle or car driving through the scene. But when Swamiji spoke, he was perfect on the first take every time. Listening to him was astral and breathtaking, even more inspiring than his usual talks. I sometimes felt as if Babaji were sitting under a tree speaking, as his enthralled disciples listened in rapt stillness.

The filmmaker asked him very insightful questions and thus prompted him to give the most brilliant answers. Swamiji was impressed with the man asking the questions — he said it was this man's unwavering attention and intelligence that drew those answers from him.

One afternoon he said something totally stunning and important for me: Speaking of Master, he said, "I have to consciously pass on his power to others." The word "consciously" caught my ear. It's not enough to think of being a light in the world for Master. Each one of us must learn to *consciously* pass on to all whom we meet his power coming through us.

The days were full to overflowing as Swamiji moved from one recording area to another. The film crew was very professional and impressive. They filmed Swamiji in the gazebo, the Temple, outside the Temple, up by the fountain, under the forest trees, up on the hillside behind the Temple, in his backyard, and in Assisi near the Basilica of St. Francis.

It was a blessed experience to walk the streets of Assisi with Swamiji, often arm in arm. The blessings were flowing boundlessly as I'd also been able to be at Swamiji's side for all the recordings and for some of the filming. In one of the film clips in Assisi, Anand, Kirtani, Narayani, Nandini, and I are with him. He was in a constant state of bliss and it was flowing to all of us. Since we'd arrived in Italy this time, it felt as if he was enfolded in softness and deep sweetness all the time.

Swamiji wrote the following words in his book, *The Promise of Immortality*:

Divine power is the perspective that accompanies greatly heightened awareness. . . . It takes power to become a son of God! . . . No one can achieve sainthood if he clings to his accustomed, human state of awareness. . . .

One who loves God deeply will speak little of his love, but will listen to the Beloved's silent whispers in his soul. . . .

And the same is true in our relationship with a master. That seeker receives most who communes in inner silence, being little interested in outward speech.

Let us speak little, then, but love much. And let us ever commune ecstatically with the Lord, as the great masters do, in our souls.

~ ~ ~ ~ ~ ~ ~ ~ ~ ~

When we were living in Gurgaon, India, with Swamiji, we'd often have staff meetings on Tuesday nights. This particular Tuesday, about mid-afternoon, we all received text messages from Dharmadas and Nirmala saying that instead of the staff meeting there would be a movie at Swamiji's house. Everyone arrived expecting to go upstairs for a movie, when suddenly Swamiji shifted gears. At that time he was writing *Revelations of Christ*, based on Master's commentaries on the New Testament. The beauty and depth of this book is breathtaking. On this evening, instead of a movie, Swamiji decided to read us Chapter 8 of the new book. All of our staff gathered to fill the living room. I could feel the energy changing—as if we were all experiencing a unique blessing. After some questions and answers at the end of the reading, Swamiji said, "Let's meditate." Everyone quickly sat upright, closed their eyes, and became aware that an opportunity of a lifetime was occurring. To meditate with Swamiji is a deep and wondrous blessing. He ended with a beautiful prayer that seemed to be simply a continuation of his inner communion with the Masters.

~ ~ ~ ~ ~ ~ ~ ~ ~ ~

In spring of 2006 Swamiji returned to the U.S. after having been away for some time, stopping first to visit in Palo Alto. Then, after years away, he was eager to return once again to his home in Crystal Hermitage. When he arrived at Ananda Village, the entire community had gathered in "downtown" Ananda to welcome him by singing "Lift Your Hearts." Swamiji was very tired at this point, so he left fairly quickly to continue on to the Hermitage. There, he asked Jyotish to park in the upper parking area, near the Shrine of the Masters, so he could walk slowly through the gardens down to his home. Swamiji paused in the Chapel and sat for a few minutes in silence.

Each year for the previous several years, the Hermitage staff, at Swamiji's request, had planted tulips in the gardens. These tulips — over 12,000 of them each year — bloomed in April, while Swamiji was traveling elsewhere. Now, for the first time he saw the lovely tulip garden, offering him an astral welcome. He walked slowly and appreciatively down through the gardens. As he entered Crystal Hermitage, he went into each room and gently touched something there. At long last he was home, and here he rested for some days.

Swamiji celebrated a very special eightieth birthday weekend at the Village that year. He gave classes on Friday and Saturday mornings. The Friday morning talk took place in the outdoor amphitheater. It was a beautiful, perfect day of sunshine, and Swamiji was radiant — almost translucent. That afternoon at the Hermitage we celebrated with the biggest birthday cake you've ever seen, and a very special gift combining elegant beauty and divine love.

Friday evening featured a performance of *The Jewel in the Lotus*, a play written by Swamiji years earlier, directed by Devi, and featuring Jyotish as the storyteller/disciple. The entire cast was magnificent. Swamiji was so deeply moved he was unable to speak afterwards.

Swamiji's birthday celebration in Ananda Village.

Rain forced us into the community center for the Saturday morning class. Swamiji began by reading a letter from Wayne Palmer (Biraj) about some new land he had just found in India. The letter was so full of enthusiasm that when Swamiji had finished reading, he asked if others in the room would like to help this project by donating an acre of the new land. By the end of the weekend, he had raised everything he needed to buy twenty-three acres (at about $20,000/acre).

Swamiji continued by saying that the work in India could be four times as big as all of our work in the West. He said that India is the homeland and it is India's destiny to be the guru of the world. When he spoke of the wonderful devotees in India whose devotion pulls him there, Swamiji's voice cracked with emotion.

The class was especially noteworthy for his having taught us how to die. He taught us so many things over these many years: how to meditate, how to be in our spines, to love one another, to be kind when we don't want to be, to build communities where we can have the support to practice these teachings. In his class that day, Swamiji stated:

"Your destiny is very high. Never put yourself down. You should all try to become *jivan muktas*. Learn to love, learn to be innocent, learn to be kind."

Saturday evening was a performance of the Oratorio by a group of about sixteen singers who had recently toured several Ananda communities and taken the music to a new level of expression and understanding. So much joy, it was hard not to weep through the entire performance.

The Sunday service was given by Jyotish and Devi, because Swamiji was tired by the end of the big weekend. But he did come to the lunchtime banquet at the Expanding Light dining room. (The crowd spilled out into the surrounding outdoors.) Swamiji looked a bit weak, but more radiant than ever. He spoke briefly, expressing with deep emotion how moved he was to see Master's light in so many eyes. And how this was the best birthday present anyone could receive.

Then he started to walk around the room, wherever there was a tiny opening between tables. I thought he would surely fall, given the many obstacles in front of him. But he moved around unerringly wherever he could squeeze in, and as he walked, the room fell silent. Each table at a time rose to greet him, and he greeted every individual he could personally, holding their hand, touching their cheek, or just gazing deeply into their eyes. The darshan took your breath away. Then, when he couldn't find any more openings through which to walk, he pronamed to everyone, standing at this point. Slowly, ever so slowly, he walked out of the dining room. He was slightly bent over, surrounded on all sides by taller heads, also slightly bent forward in homage.

CHAPTER 12

Renunciation

Swamiji had survived the Bhrigu predictions that he would die in his eighty-third year (see the chapter "Living for God") and now, a few months into that year, he was his usual superhuman, creative self. It was a blessed time because he was busy writing about the new renunciate order. He had started this task some months earlier, after his miraculous recovery on his return to Assisi from Lugano, and was now in the process of finishing the book, called *A Renunciate Order for the New Age*.

When Swamiji was writing a book, he often would have anyone who visited read the latest pages he had written. One day he asked me to read the final chapter. I couldn't believe it, but for some reason I wept uncontrollably while reading the first four pages. Swamiji was as surprised as I was, and wanted to know what was going on. The only thing I could think was that I had broken my vows to God in other lifetimes and some part of me remembered the pain of that separation. The following morning when Swamiji had me read the rest of that chapter, which contained the actual vows to God, I wept again. It was all rather embarrassing, but he and I had a very good talk about it. Swamiji told me that God's grace could and would do everything. All I had to do was keep striving every day in every way. He also suggested that I do more chanting to help strengthen my devotion, as this was what I needed.

Later that day I wrote Swamiji the following email:

Dear Swamiji,

The last chapter is moving beyond words, as you witnessed. The tears are of the joy of hope but also of a deep anguish of self-doubt. The question that always plagues me is how deep is my devotion? How firm is my commitment to finding God in this lifetime? There's no doubt that the climb must be made, death is clearly the only alternative, but it does seem that I tarry a great deal on the less steep parts of the path.

I'm so grateful for you, Swamiji, for all that you've done and for this new renunciate order. It always must be "more and deeper," and we're so blessed that you're always there by our sides, urging us on, to fight the good fight.

Please pray that God bless me with the deep yearning in my heart for Him, and Him alone.

at your feet in His love,
Miriam

Immediately after finishing the book, Swamiji decided to have the first vow ceremony in Ananda Assisi. He would initiate these first renunciates himself. Swamiji called the spiritual directors from around the world and a few of the others he felt were ready for vows of complete renunciation and asked them to come to Assisi for the ceremony. It was a time of excitement, confusion, and questioning among many who felt in their hearts that they might be ready to make their vow of renunciation to God and Guru.

Below is an excerpt from a letter that Cecilia Sharma, an Italian devotee, sent out at the time. She is wonderfully expressive, and her letter conveys the emotions and feelings that were being stirred up at that time.

Dear ones,

May the pure silence of this Italian night resonate within our hearts, with the peace of the twinkling light of all the stars now adorning as an aura of diamonds these blessed hills of Assisi! . . .

The book suddenly was completed ten days ago, when before people could even realize that such a gift was there, the first Ceremony unexpectedly was announced by Swamiji and was to be led by himself!

You can imagine how everybody here felt! And how each one is feeling!

Each future tyagi, brahmachari, nayaswami: so many questions, doubts, unclear visions, little fears and more questions! [Calmness came that day as] Swamiji specified that these extraordinary affirmations are *directional* for a lifetime, inclusive, expansive, and nonsectarian. . . .

A strong call to us, but in an expanded way, as well, as clearly written within the vows: to reach out in love and service *to all humanity*.

And *to be channels of blessings to all mankind.*

There is a thrilling Joy in the air, and the feeling of a special Grace which is already glowing. . . .

God bless you all!
Cecilia and Vivek AUM AUM AUM!

I wondered which vow was appropriate for me, because I was married to Dharana Brown, who was living in India. He and I discussed this via email quite extensively, and we decided it was most appropriate as a couple to take the vow of tyaga. Then Dharana wrote his own letter personally to Swamiji. After much prayer, anguish, and meditation, I changed my mind and felt strongly to take the vow of complete renunciation, as you can see from this letter that I wrote to Swamiji:

Dear Swamiji,

I've struggled so much in these past days since reading the renunciate vows for the first time. They've made my heart and soul sing while at the same time I've experienced a strange grief in reading and studying them. I've introspected over my initial response to the chapter on vows of renunciation. Both the joy and the grief are profound. I believe now that the tears of grief stem from the memory of breaking my vows to God in, most probably, countless past lives. There was and remains a deep pain in the memory of such a separation from God. You wrote, "the Lord Himself, and His angels, come to your assistance," and to consciously separate myself from such a blessing has brought a seemingly endless anguish.

However, Swamiji, after much thought and prayer, I'd like to try again in this lifetime.

Swamiji, although my heart most resonates with the Vow of Complete Renunciation, I was thinking to ask for the Vow of Tyaga. However, this morning when I spoke with Anand, he told me that he thought it was appropriate, if I so desired, to ask for the Vow of Complete Renunciation. I've read and reread this vow countless times and have to admit that I experience difficulty breathing when I consider the breadth and height of such an undertaking. Anand reminded me that these vows are directional. You said the same thing to me the other day.

Swamiji, if you see, in this bundle of self-definitions, the potential to "have no goal in life but to know Thee, and to serve as Thy channel of blessing to all mankind," I'd like very much to take the Vow of Complete Renunciation next week.

at your feet in love and gratitude,
Miriam

After reading my letter, and also the letter from Dharana, Swamiji came out of his office the next morning, looked directly into my eyes, and said, most determinedly, "I will *make* you a nayaswami, and Dharana can become a tyagi." I felt I was rocking back and forth between a state of grace and a state of shock. But now with Swamiji's determined energy behind me, there could be no confusion or doubt. I was just stepping up to bat. Swamiji was the one who would be hitting the ball.

November 20, 2009, was the big day, and as you can imagine, it was quite intense. We had a three-hour meditation that morning with only those who would be taking vows later that day. There were at least forty people in the Temple, maybe more. It was an unguided meditation, and Kirtani had all three of the vows read in both Italian and English. She had handed me the Vow of Complete Renunciation while we were preparing for meditation and asked if I could read it without my glasses. I thought she meant just read it to myself, and I said yes. However, when things commenced I realized that I was the one who would read it aloud to everyone. I became quite nervous, but since I was last, I had some time to calm down. I started off reading as though I was reading to everyone in the Temple. Then I realized that this vow is spoken directly to God. With this realization, the energy in my voice changed.

It was amazing to see how much could get stirred up inside with the decision to take a step of complete renunciation. The ego (mine)

Swamiji with the new nayaswamis.

was quite uncomfortable. Wonderfully, though, that morning Swamiji let me give him a footbath and take care of his feet. I was blessed beyond measure to be in his intimate presence so many times a day, and especially this day.

In the afternoon, we gathered in the Temple of Light for meditation to prepare for the ceremony. When Swamiji arrived to begin the initiation, the Temple was packed to the walls. Instead of the usual arrangement where everyone sits facing the altar, now we all sat in large concentric circles around a central fire ring that had been prepared for the nayaswami fire ceremony. Those taking nayaswami vows sat in the circle closest to the fire, with the prospective tyagis and brahmacharis in the next rows. Anyone else from the community was welcome to attend to offer their energy and prayers for this important event.

Swamiji gave a beautiful talk about this new order. Now that we are in Dwapara Yuga, it offers a positive concept of renunciation—with the focus on the joy you are embracing rather than on what you are renouncing. The evening was deeply moving; Swamiji's voice often broke with feeling as he read the vows for us to repeat.

The tyagis and brahmacharis took their vows first and the nayaswamis last, saying their vows as part of a fire ceremony. After we had repeated the nayaswami vows, Swamiji asked all of the nayaswamis to make a full body prostration towards the fire. This was an especially moving experience, to feel the entire front of my body and face pressed to the ground with the arms and hands outstretched overhead offering myself to God without reservation.

Lila, Lakshman, and I, who were part of Swamiji's daily life and traveling entourage, all became nayaswamis that evening. It seemed important that Swamiji be surrounded by renunciates in these final years of his life. Narayani, who was to join our staff the following year, took her vow of brahmacharya that same evening.

Those first three years of being a sannyasi felt natural and blessed. As the years passed, I began to wonder if I could maintain the vow of complete renunciation once Swamiji was no longer in the body. But certainly, as long as I was serving him, I would remain a nayaswami. I also realized during this time that my marriage with Dharana was finished, and we eventually divorced.

Early in 2013, Narayani, Shurjo, and I, at Swamiji's request, were making plans to take him to the Himalayas, where he would spend the remainder of his life in seclusion. But this was not to happen. Swamiji passed away in April 2013.

After Swamiji's passing, I felt deeply called to move to our new Ananda community, Ananda Laurelwood, outside of Portland, Oregon. For the next five years I helped to develop a retreat center there. My role was a very outward one, in which I worked closely with the many men and women who were a part of that work.

It was my intention to remain a nayaswami for at least one year after Swamiji's passing. I felt a relationship was coming and I wanted to renounce the vow before it showed up. So, in the summer of 2014, I met with Jyotish and Devi. I was in great anguish over this decision because here I was once again breaking my vow to God. But they were so kind and loving. Jyotish said immediately that it is not about the outer form of renunciation but rather the inner renunciation. He told me that I'd obviously been a nun or a monk in many lifetimes and I knew how to live that way. But now I needed to learn how to live these teachings in the world. Devi was very insightful in pointing out that Swamiji needed all of us who were close around him in those final years to be renunciates. But now I needed to move on to the next step on my spiritual path. They blessed me at the spiritual eye and at the heart. I wept. In an effort to help lighten the mood so I wouldn't take myself so seriously, Devi looked back as they were walking away and said, "Miriam, keep your blue clothes. You can always take the vow again when you're eighty!"

Several months after renouncing my vow, I saw the man I knew immediately I was to marry. He and I have been able to serve Master's work together. I love remembering the holiness of my initiation in November 2009. Even though I'm no longer outwardly a sannyasi, the vow remains a constant guide in my spiritual life.

~ ~ ~ ~ ~ ~ ~ ~ ~

Vow of Complete Renunciation

From now on, I embrace as the only purpose of my life the search for God.

I will never take a partner, or, if I am married, I will look upon my partner as belonging only to Thee, Lord. In any case, I am complete in myself, and in myself will merge all the opposites of duality.

I no longer exist as a separate entity, but offer my life unreservedly into Thy great Ocean of Awareness.

I accept nothing as mine, no one as mine, no talent, no success, no achievement as my own, but everything as Thine alone.

I will feel that not only the fruit of my labor, but the labor itself, is only Thine. Act through me always, Lord, to accomplish Thy design.

I am free in Thy joy, and will rejoice forever in Thy blissful presence.

Help me in my efforts to achieve perfection in this, my holy vow. For I have no goal in life but to know Thee, and to serve as Thy channel of blessing to all mankind.

CHAPTER 13

Vanished the Veils of Light and Shade

It had been over a year that Swamiji had been away from India. Now, in 2011, he was once again in the beautiful home that had been built for him on the Pune land. As we saw so often in his life, any time the light became strong, the darkness tried to drive it out. Swamiji's body was often the battlefield for the war between darkness and light.

During this time, he became ill with several unrelated symptoms. Neither Dr. Peter nor I felt clear about what was happening. The lab results showed he was in kidney failure; but he had chronic renal failure and those test results didn't look any worse than usual. He was having severe pain in his left foot, which was obviously gout. And then things got darker. Within just a few hours, Swamiji began passing black stool. In the same moment, a black cat, a rat, and a bat all appeared in his house. We managed to get these animals of ill omen out of the house.

Even more disturbing than the symptoms and the ill omens was a strange feeling in the air. In the past, when Swamiji's health crashed, I seemed always to know what to do next, and with Dr. Peter's help we could move forward. But this time, nothing seemed obvious. I stood in front of Master's photo and begged him to tell me what to do. The only thing I could hear was, "Get Swamiji off the land." We didn't have a doctor or hospital set up for his care in Pune. All we could think to do was take Swamiji to his favorite hotel, Le Meridien, in Pune city.

I called Brahmachari Aditya Gait, one of our monks who has experience in the medical field, and asked for recommendations for a hospital and doctor for Swamiji. Aditya knew an Ananda devotee in her first year of residency at a hospital in Pune and had her call me. When she understood the situation, Dr. Mansi Aggarwal took matters into her own hands. She made arrangements for Swamiji to be seen by the top critical care physician in the hospital where she was doing her residency. After we checked Swamiji into the hotel, we went to the emergency room of Deenanath Mangeshkar Hospital to see Dr. Jog Sameer Arvind, head of Intensive Care.

We were accustomed to the beautiful Max Super specialty Hospital in New Delhi, which had been built to cater to medical tourism for Westerners. This hospital was clearly for the local people. To us it seemed dark and dingy. There were several hundred people milling about its huge open reception area. The emergency room itself was even darker and dingier.

We met Dr. Jog and I liked him immediately—he had a light in his eyes and was obviously keenly intelligent. He said Swamiji needed to be admitted to the hospital for further tests. Swamiji did not care for hospitals; usually I was able to treat his medical conditions at home and sometimes in hotel rooms. We agreed that we would take Swamiji back to the hotel and return the next morning for more tests. They promised us one of their VIP rooms. I had high hopes for this VIP room!

We took Swamiji back to the hospital the next day and were admitted into a VIP room. It too was dark and dingy, and Narayani and I were struggling with what to do. There were many medical students in their first, second, and third year of residency who began moving around Swamiji to do various tests. One very important test involved drawing blood from an artery to check blood gases. Unfortunately, the third-year resident was unable to access the artery on his first or second attempt. I told him firmly that he had only one more try and he had better succeed this time. Fortunately, he did succeed and left the room with his blood sample. He and several others of the medical students came back very quickly and told us they needed to move Swamiji into the Intensive Care Unit. I still wasn't convinced this was the right place for Swamiji and was holding to my promise to him to avoid hospitals and take care of him myself with the help of Dr. Peter Van Houten, advising me over the phone from the U.S. When the medical residents realized they weren't getting anywhere with me, they went to get the top man.

Dr. Jog arrived and was very kind. He asked to speak to me privately. In the hallway, he began to enumerate the many intravenous medications he needed to give Swamiji. As a cardiac care nurse, I knew that every one of those medications had to be given under strict surveillance in a critical care unit. I asked Dr. Jog, "Will you take Swamiji away from us?" I explained that in the U.S., when a patient is placed in intensive care the family can only visit a few times a day, for very short periods of time. Dr. Jog said, "Come with me." He moved very quickly; we ran down six flights of stairs and he burst through the main doors of the Intensive Care Unit. We walked

Swamiji in India after his illness.

quickly to the back of the unit into an empty room that was clearly prepared and waiting for Swamiji. He said, "This is where I want to put Swamiji, and that is your room." He pointed to a door to a small room with a cot, which was the family's room. Every room in the Intensive Care Unit has an adjoining room where the family can stay. Each of those family rooms has a door that leads into a hallway, so family can enter their rooms without going through the intensive care unit. Dr. Jog told me they understand the importance of family in the healing process. I started crying.

I found my way back to Swamiji's room. Although Swamiji was very weak and not speaking at all, I knew he was conscious. I felt he needed to make this decision himself. I knelt by his bed so I could speak into his good ear. I said, "Swamiji, if you think your time has come, we will take you home and let you go peacefully. But if this is not the time, we need to have you admitted to the Intensive Care Unit."

Swamiji opened his eyes and seemed to think about this proposition. Then he took a deep breath and said, "I have an obligation to stay in this body as long as I can to serve Master's work." I looked up at all the medical residency students standing around his bed and nodded, "Yes." They immediately grabbed his bed and ran for the elevator. As we were about to charge through the doors of the Intensive Care unit, one of them motioned to me and said, "You go that way," and Narayani and I took that little outer hallway that led to the family room adjoining Swamiji's room. Thanks to that little room, Narayani and I never left Swamiji's side.

The medical team began urgently working on Swamiji. And they did not stop working on him for twenty-four hours hours straight. His kidneys were in complete failure and he would not have lived for many more days without dialysis. It took them all that time to stabilize the body enough to ready him for it. Once the dialysis was started, the critical state of Swamiji's condition became even more apparent. For the next several hours his heart rhythm was extremely unstable and at any moment could have become life threatening. I was glued to the heart monitor and constantly making sure the medical staff was aware of what was happening! They reassured me again and again that this was simply a difficult moment and they were doing everything possible to reverse the situation. Fortunately, the dialysis was successful and Swamiji's own kidneys were able to take over their function again; his heart rhythm stabilized.

Swamiji was in the ICU for several days. He underwent many procedures that were quite painful. At times he spoke openly about taking on the karma of specific Ananda devotees and the work in Pune. He stated that he felt it was an important part of his work. He also reaffirmed many times throughout those days, "I'm happy to do it."

CHAPTER 14

The Soul Is Untouched

In the last few years of his life, Swamiji continued to have health challenges. Yet we continued to see that time and again, even though Swamiji could be experiencing intense symptoms, they would cease the moment he arrived for a scheduled event. Oftentimes he would be quite ill right up to the moment he either walked onto the stage with assistance or was taken up in a wheelchair. As soon as the microphone was placed in front of him, all health problems ceased to exist.

In the last eight months of his life, Swamiji toured several major cities in India — New Delhi, Kolkata, Pune, Mumbai, Bangalore,

Swamiji speaking at Siri Fort.

and Chennai — giving discourses to thousands of people. One of his biggest physical challenges then was the ability of his kidneys to function properly. After visiting several cities between the months of September and January, Swamiji took a vacation to Goa. He wanted only Narayani and Shurjo with him in the hotel, so I stayed at another hotel a little way down the beach. Swamiji's kidney function was so dangerously low that I warned him he might have to cancel his talk in Chennai in order to return to Pune and get dialysis.

I planned to take another lab sample from Swamiji in a few days, but he gave me a call and asked me to come do the test that morning. The following day's report from the lab came as a shock. I called Dr. Peter in the U.S. and told him the results were too good to be true. Swamiji's kidneys had vastly improved in function. I called Narayani and told her to tell Swamiji that he was going to Chennai!

Within a few days, Swamiji lost the water weight resulting from the poor kidney function, and he was visibly improved. We embarked for Chennai, where the event was to be held in an enormous auditorium that seated two thousand. The auditorium was full to capacity, with standing room only. There were another five hundred people out in a large hallway where they could watch Swamiji on monitors mounted at either end. The only place I could find to sit was on the floor, almost under the stage. I couldn't see Swamiji, but I could hear him. I had my nurse's mind going and was analyzing how he was doing. In my assessment, he was obviously fatigued, and I was worried. Then I realized that those two thousand people sitting in the auditorium were so quiet you could have heard a pin drop. They were all hanging on Swamiji's every word. I stopped listening with my nurse's mind and tuned in to Swamiji's vibration and energy. It was stunning. He had the entire

Swamiji with Sri Kaarthikeyan (far left) and others from Ananda India.

auditorium completely wrapped in an aura of divine love. I was so deeply moved, I wept.

Swamiji had demonstrated once again that he was not the body. He was pure consciousness. Divine Love.

~ ~ ~ ~ ~ ~ ~ ~ ~ ~

When he learned that I was writing this book, Sri Kaarthikeyan sent me the following, which he was kind enough to allow me to include:

On the personal request of Swami Kriyananda, I accompanied him on his last visits to the major cities in India.

In each city I would introduce Swamiji before his talk. In Chennai we were in the prestigious Musical Academy Hall that was overflowing with devotees. Even Swamiji was moved. In spite of his indisposition, he made a powerful speech. Several hundreds were standing outside to listen to him. Later that evening at dinner I said to Swamiji, "There is a great impact of your visit to Chennai. Maybe during your next visit we will organize the function in the larger Indore stadium." Swami responded, "Mr. Kaarthikeyan, I don't think this body will allow that." It seems Swamiji had the premonition that this would be his last visit to India.

D.R. Kaarthikeyan

CHAPTER 15

The Final Exam

In the last few weeks of Swamiji's life, it was becoming clearer and clearer that he wanted to leave this physical plane. Over the years he'd often talked about being ready to leave the body, but there always seemed to be one more project he needed to complete. Now, however, as we see in letters to some of his close friends, he'd lost all enthusiasm for living. His health challenges were encroaching more and more on his ability to function as he wished. He had served for years from a state of exhaustion, with great fatigue in his heart. Now there were fewer things he could do well or at all on the physical plane. Swamiji wrote the following Easter message, sent out March 29, 2013:

Dear Ones:

I wish I could bless each and every one of you with a happy Easter. Easter is a time symbolizing the eventual resurrection of our little, individual selves into the one, Infinite Self. I suggest at this time particularly that you study and meditate on the photograph of Master titled

The Last Smile. And consider this amazing fact: He knew that in just a few moments he would be leaving his physical body forever! There is no thought of self in his eyes, of personal regret, of sorrow. Clearly visible in his eyes and in his facial expression is his unconditional love for all mankind; his readiness to return "again and again," as he put it, as long as one stray brother sits weeping by the wayside. Such love, for ego-centered humanity, is not even conceivable. And this was the love Jesus, too, felt for all humanity. People weep for him and his suffering on the cross. His suffering was only for humanity, that blindly rejects God's love and substitutes for it vengefulness and hatred!

I have been going through a personal Armageddon. Nothing in this world attracts me anymore. Nothing at all holds any pleasant memories — none of those experiences, whether interpersonal or outward in any way, holds the slightest attraction for me. Must I really live another five years, as has been predicted for me? I confess the very idea appalls me.

I have done so much in my life to please God. The very hallmark of my nature has been enthusiasm, even though I've been always aware that I could never really accomplish anything significant in this world. Suddenly, now, I feel bereft of that enthusiasm. Maybe it's because my heart feels very tired. I want only to merge in God. The only lingering thought is that I would like to bring all of you with me. No, I am far from tired of you! I want only your freedom in God. But no, your worldly attachments, identities, and desires, I have to confess mean simply nothing to me, as my own mean nothing to me.

No, this doesn't mean I love you less. I love you much more, for I love that part of you which is eternally real.

But whether I succeed or fail in my projects is to me meaningless. All the things I once considered pleasurable are to me, now, displeasing. I want nothing that this world has to offer. People tell me I am famous: that phrase, to me, also is meaningless. People often marvel at all I have been able to accomplish in this life: to me, it all seems only dust.

If we must resurrect our souls, let it be from the delusion that anything in this cosmic dream holds some worthwhile reality for us. We are children of God: That is our sole reality!

Love,
swami

In the week before he passed, Swamiji became much more inward. He wasn't having people over for tea and spent most of his time either alone or in the company only of Narayani and Shurjo. Swamiji wrote the following letter ten days before he passed and sent it to some of his closest friends. Note the last paragraph (always another project to expand Master's work!):

Dear Ones:

Despite those two ancient prophecies, both of which said I would live to be 91, I am beginning to wonder if I'll even make it to my 87th birthday next month. My heart is very tired, and has been so for days and days. After my heart surgery on Dec. 18, 1994, it became impossible for me to practice Kriya anymore; my breathing became too shallow. Now it seems to be more like panting than breathing—so much so, it's difficult even to sleep. Night after night I lie awake, unable to rest properly.

Please understand, I'm not complaining. Rather, I rather look forward to leaving this body. But I wanted you to know that, even though I may still live to be 91, at the moment it sure doesn't seem probable. Maybe Master feels I have done enough now. Whatever be the case, I thought you should know. And Dick, though you've sometimes addressed me scoldingly for not living by your standards, I want you to know that I have always been fond of you.

Maybe my strength will come back. I'm willing that it should. But I'm equally willing that it shouldn't. Right now, I can barely do anything. Even digesting my food has become a chore!

Well, on to another subject: that magazine, Shivani, in Finding Happiness, "Profiles," seems like an excellent name for a magazine. Could we start one? It could cover countless subjects, and in fascinating ways. If we decide to give it a try, who could head up such a project?

Love to all of you,
swami

A few days before he passed, he wanted to go into town to do a little shopping. He went to some of his favorite shops and visited with the shop owners who had been his acquaintances for many years. The day before he passed, he invited some of his closest friends at Ananda Assisi over for tea.

Swamiji often had a difficult time sleeping at night. He had also complained for years about how tired his heart felt. During our morning chat about his health a few days before he passed, he told me he had once again been unable to sleep. He said that he had gotten up instead and meditated for three hours. For someone who had not slept, he looked radiant and glowing.

The morning of his passing seemed like every other morning except that he was still asleep when I arrived there at 7. Often, if he couldn't sleep during the night, he would fall asleep around 5 a.m. and sleep until 7 a.m. Jaidhara, his cook, was in the kitchen as usual and had decided to make Swamiji pancakes this morning. Narayani and I went downstairs for our regular morning discussion about Swamiji. Around 7:30 we heard him moving upstairs and she quickly went up. I followed close on her heels.

Swamiji had gotten out of bed, dressed himself in his light-blue bathrobe, and walked to his computer to check e-mails as was his habit. He checked his e-mails frequently to see if anyone needed his help in any way. When I walked into the dining room, which was also his office, he was still sitting in his desk chair. I asked my usual morning question, "Swamiji, how are you?" He looked very pale, and simply shrugged his shoulders in response. It was not uncommon for him to be less than enthusiastic about seeing the nurse in the morning, so I went into the kitchen to see how the pancakes were coming along.

Narayani came into the kitchen after she had been with Swamiji for a few minutes; she felt something was wrong and wanted me to check him again. When I returned to the dining room, he was seated at the table seemingly waiting for breakfast. I asked him how he was feeling. He looked at Narayani and said, "What is she saying?" I moved closer to his right ear and said more loudly, "Swamiji, can you hear me?" He once again looked at Narayani and said, "What is she saying?" I then asked if I could test his blood sugar to make sure he wasn't in a hypoglycemic state. His response to the question was, "Anything." I took his blood sugar and it was normal. I told Narayani that he must just be having a bad morning and left the room.

Narayani immediately called me back and said, "Something's wrong." When I came back into the room, nothing seemed to be happening, but then very quickly Swamiji began to have a small seizure. His hands and arms were clenching up towards his chest, his jaw was clenched, and his face became a dusky rose color. I told Narayani to call Narya, so she stepped out of the room to find her phone. I wrapped my arms around Swamiji's upper body to help keep him in the chair and also to try to palpate his heartbeat between the ribs of his left chest. The seizure lasted only a few seconds, and then suddenly Swamiji slumped down in his chair, his arms relaxed. He had stopped breathing and I could not feel his heartbeat.

Jaidhara walked into the room, and I told him to race to the Temple immediately to get Anand and Kirtani. All color had drained from Swamiji's face, and he had the pallor I have seen many times in those who have passed. As Narayani walked back into the room, I looked at her and said, "He's dying." Adamantly she cried, "No! No, it's not time yet!" Since I trust her intuition, I thought that perhaps if we chanted AUM in his right ear we could bring him back. I tried to do the AUMs but my voice was choked up with tears. At this point Shurjo entered the room and I told him to chant AUM in Swamiji's right ear. His AUMs were deep and resonant, and in a few seconds Swamiji started to breathe again, his color returned, and I could feel a very rapid heartbeat between the ribs of his chest.

The three of us were easily able to drag the chair with Swamiji in it into his bedroom. We lifted him onto the bed and positioned him so he could breathe more easily. Shurjo continued to chant AUM in his right ear and I was telling Swamiji to breathe. Anand and Kirtani arrived; I told Kirtani that he had almost left, but AUM brought him back. I asked her please to call Jyotish and Devi to tell them what was happening.

We tried to reposition Swamiji onto his left side to help him breathe. But this didn't seem to work so we turned him again onto his back. I told Narayani to change places with me and tell him to breathe, because I thought he might listen to her voice better than to mine.

As she said, "Swami, breathe!" he opened his eyes about halfway and looked at her from a far, faraway place. He looked directly at her, then closed his eyes, and took his last breath with a very long exhale. His breathing stopped and there was no longer a heartbeat. Kirtani was in another room on the phone with Jyotish and Devi. I went to get her so she could be at Swamiji's side. We all knelt on the floor around Swamiji's bed for several minutes as Shurjo continued to chant AUM into Swamiji's right ear. Then he stopped, and we all sat in the silence and stillness. There was a powerful feeling of Swamiji's omnipresence permeating and emanating throughout the room. Then Kirtani led us in chanting AUM to Swamiji's soul for several minutes.

Others began arriving at the house and came in to sit quietly and meditate with Swamiji's body. Then, we needed to prepare Swamiji's body to be taken to the Temple of Light. Kirtani, Shivani, Narayani, and I washed his body with lavender scented water and dressed him in his blue nayaswami robe. Jaidhara and Shurjo picked flower petals from outside the house and brought them in to put around Swamiji's body. More people continued to come and sit with Swamiji.

This continued in his house for a period of about two hours. Then the time came to transport Swamiji's body to the Temple. He was placed in the back of Anand's station wagon and Bryan (Aryavan), Jaidhara, Shurjo, and Jayadev rode with him. Swamiji's body was placed in the Temple on an area that had been specially prepared with beautiful altar cloths and flowers. As word spread throughout the community, devotees began to gather quietly in the Temple to pray and chant together. Jayadev and Kirtani led one chant after another as people quietly came forward with flowers and tears to pay homage to a soul that many considered to be their very best friend. After a few hours, Kirtani led the astral ascension ceremony.

Swamiji's body remained on the special altar all the rest of the day and into the afternoon of the next. He was then placed into a casket on Monday afternoon. There were people with him night and day, sometimes in quiet prayer and meditation, at other times chanting or sharing stories of how Swamiji had touched and changed our lives forever. Swamiji's body remained in the Temple in the open casket for eight days as people from all over the world gathered to pay tribute. It was a time of profound grief in the midst of great waves of Swamiji's omnipresent love and joy. In those days, we were able to be with his body all day and all night, touching his hands, his feet, and lovingly caressing his radiant face. Many people felt Swamiji very near, could almost hear him laughing and see him as youthful, vibrant, and enthusiastic. There was, indeed, joy in the heavens! Jai Guru! Jai Swamiji!

Goodbye, Swamiji.

Epilogue

In 2006 we wanted to do something special for Swamiji's fifty-eighth Spiritual Anniversary of discipleship to Master. We transformed the living room at Guru Kripa, his home in Gurgaon, India, into an astral wonderland. Though we invited only "staff," with a small number of Americans and a large number of Indians, mostly volunteers, the living room was packed! Swamiji read from *The New*

*Swamiji's final resting place, the Moksha Mandir,
at Ananda Village in Nevada City, California.*

Path about meeting Master on September 12 more than half a century earlier. His voice would break from time to time with emotion, and by the end there probably wasn't a dry eye in the room. It felt like each of us had come to Master on that auspicious day and been accepted as his disciple. Swamiji's story is our story too.

Swamiji invited questions and there were many. Someone asked about the time Swamiji had asked Master if he would be with us as much after his death as he was then. So Swamiji told us the story, ending with Master's words, "For those who think me near, I will be near." Then a very dear, sweet voice piped up and asked Swamiji, "Will *you* be with us as much after you're gone?" Swamiji stumbled over his words for a moment, then clearly said, "If I achieve what I hope to achieve, I will be with you, yes. Yes."

Dear Reader,

Ananda is a worldwide work based on the teachings expressed in this book—those of the great spiritual teacher, Paramhansa Yogananda. If you enjoyed this title, Crystal Clarity Publishers invites you to continue to deepen your spiritual life through the many avenues of Ananda Worldwide—including meditation communities, centers, and groups; online virtual community and webinars; retreat centers offering classes and teacher training in yoga and meditation; and more.

For special offers and discounts for first-time visitors to Ananda, visit us online at crystalclarity.com.

Feel free to contact us. We are here to serve you.

Joy to you,

Crystal Clarity Publishers

ANANDA WORLDWIDE

Ananda, a worldwide organization founded by Swami Kriyananda, offers spiritual support and resources based on the teachings of Paramhansa Yogananda. There are Ananda spiritual communities in Nevada City, Sacramento, and Palo Alto, California; Seattle, Washington; and Portland, Oregon; as well as a retreat center and European community in Assisi, Italy. Ananda supports more than 140 meditation groups worldwide, including many in India that are expanding rapidly.

For more information about Ananda's work, our communities, or meditation groups near you, please call 530-478-7560 or visit ananda.org.

THE EXPANDING LIGHT RETREAT

The Expanding Light is the largest retreat center in the world to share exclusively the teachings of Paramhansa Yogananda. Situated in the Ananda Village community, it offers the opportunity to experience spiritual life in a contemporary ashram setting. The varied, year-round schedule of classes and programs on yoga, meditation, and spiritual practice includes Karma Yoga, Personal Retreat, Spiritual Travel, and online learning. The Ananda School of Yoga & Meditation offers certified yoga, yoga therapist, spiritual counselor, and meditation teacher trainings. Large groups are welcome.

The teaching staff are experts in Kriya Yoga meditation and all aspects of Yogananda's teachings. All staff members live at Ananda Village and bring an uplifting approach to their areas of service. The serene natural setting and delicious vegetarian meals help provide an ideal environment for a truly meaningful visit.

For more information, please contact us at:
800-346-5350   expandinglight.org

CRYSTAL CLARITY PUBLISHERS

Crystal Clarity Publishers offers many additional resources to assist you in your spiritual journey, including many other books (see the following pages for some of them), a wide variety of inspirational and relaxation music composed by Swami Kriyananda, and yoga and meditation videos. To place an order for the above products, or for more information, please contact us at:

crystalclarity.com   800-424-1055
clarity@crystalclarity.com
1123 Goodrich Blvd. / Commerce, CA 90022

Visit our website for our online catalog, with secure ordering.

FURTHER EXPLORATIONS

with Crystal Clarity

AUTOBIOGRAPHY OF A YOGI
Paramhansa Yogananda

Autobiography of a Yogi is one of the best-selling Eastern philosophy titles of all time, with millions of copies sold, named one of the best and most influential books of the twentieth century. This highly prized reprinting of the original 1946 edition is the only one available free from textual changes made after Yogananda's death. Yogananda was the first yoga master of India whose mission was to live and teach in the West.

In this updated edition are bonus materials, including a last chapter that Yogananda wrote in 1951, without posthumous changes. This new edition also includes the eulogy that Yogananda wrote for Gandhi, and a new foreword and afterword by Swami Kriyananda, one of Yogananda's close, direct disciples.

Also available in unabridged audiobook (MP3) format, read by Swami Kriyananda.

PARAMHANSA YOGANANDA
A Biography with Personal Reflections and Reminiscences
Swami Kriyananda

Paramhansa Yogananda's classic *Autobiography of a Yogi*—perhaps surprisingly, in light of his world-transforming accomplishments—is more about the saints Yogananda met than about himself.

Now, one of Yogananda's direct disciples relates the untold story of this great spiritual master and world teacher: his teenage miracles, his challenges in coming to America, his national lecture campaigns, his struggles to fulfill his world-changing mission amid incomprehension and painful betrayals, and his ultimate triumphant achievement. Kriyananda's subtle grasp of his guru's inner nature reveals Yogananda's many-sided greatness. Includes many never-before-published anecdotes.

Also available in unabridged audiobook (MP3) format, read by Swami Kriyananda.

THE NEW PATH
My Life with Paramhansa Yogananda
Swami Kriyananda

When Swami Kriyananda discovered *Autobiography of a Yogi* in 1948, he was totally new to Eastern teachings. This is a great advantage to the Western reader, since Kriyananda walks us along the yogic path as he discovers it from the moment of his initiation as a disciple of Yogananda. With winning honesty, humor, and deep insight, he shares his journey on the spiritual path through personal stories and experiences.

Through more than four hundred stories of life with Yogananda, we tune in more deeply to this great master and to the teachings he brought to the West. This book is an ideal complement to *Autobiography of a Yogi*.

Demystifying Patanjali
The Wisdom of Paramhansa Yogananda Presented by his direct disciple, Swami Kriyananda

The Essence of Self-Realization
*The Wisdom of Paramhansa Yogananda
Recorded, compiled, and edited by his disciple, Swami Kriyananda*

Conversations with Yogananda
Recorded, with Reflections, by his disciple, Swami Kriyananda

Revelations of Christ
*Proclaimed by Paramhansa Yogananda
Presented by his disciple, Swami Kriyananda*

The Essence of the Bhagavad Gita
*Explained by Paramhansa Yogananda
As remembered by his disciple, Swami Kriyananda*

Whispers from Eternity
*Paramhansa Yogananda
Edited by his disciple, Swami Kriyananda*

The Rubaiyat of Omar Khayyam Explained
*Paramhansa Yogananda
Edited by his disciple, Swami Kriyananda*

The Wisdom of Yogananda series
  How to Be Happy All the Time
  Karma and Reincarnation
  How to Love and Be Loved
  How to Be a Success
  How to Have Courage, Calmness, and Confidence
  How to Achieve Glowing Health and Vitality
  How to Achieve Your True Potential
  The Man Who Refused Heaven

Meditation for Starters with CD
Swami Kriyananda

Intuition for Starters
Swami Kriyananda

Chakras for Starters
Savitri Simpson

Vegetarian Cooking for Starters
Diksha McCord

The Art and Science of Raja Yoga
Swami Kriyananda

Awaken to Superconsciousness
Swami Kriyananda

Living Wisely, Living Well
Swami Kriyananda

The Bhagavad Gita
According to Paramhansa Yogananda
Edited by his disciple, Swami Kriyananda

How to Meditate
Jyotish Novak

Self-Expansion Through Marriage
Swami Kriyananda

The Time Tunnel
Swami Kriyananda

The Yugas
Joseph Selbie and David Steinmetz

God Is for Everyone
Inspired by Paramhansa Yogananda
As taught to and understood by his disciple, Swami
Kriyananda

Religion in the New Age
Swami Kriyananda

The Art of Supportive Leadership
J. Donald Walters (Swami Kriyananda)

Money Magnetism
J. Donald Walters (Swami Kriyananda)

Change Your Magnetism, Change Your Life
Naidhruva Rush

In Divine Friendship
Swami Kriyananda

Sharing Nature
Joseph Cornell

The Sky and Earth Touched Me
Joseph Cornell

Education for Life
J. Donald Walters (Swami Kriyananda)

The Meaning of Dreaming
Savitri Simpson

The Healing Kitchen
Diksha McCord

Love Perfected, Life Divine
Swami Kriyananda

Stand Unshaken!
Daily Inspiration for Living Fearlessly
Nayaswamis Jyotish and Devi

The Need for Spiritual Communities
Swami Kriyananda

Secrets of Meditation and Inner Peace
Swami Kriyananda